STATE FORMATION AMONG TRIBALS

A Quest for Santal Identity

State Formation Among Tribals

A Quest for Santal Identity

A.B. Chaudhuri

GYAN

Published by

GYAN

Gyan Publishing House
5, Ansari Road
Daryaganj, New Delhi-110002
Phone: 011-47034999, 9811692060
E-mail: books@gyanbooks.com

Distribution Network
gyanbooks.com
India, USA, Canada, UK, Australia, France

ISBN: 978-81-212-0422-4 (HB)

Reprint in India, 2024
First Published, 2013

Printed at: Gyan Press, Delhi.

State Formation Among Tribals: A Quest For Santal Identity
Author: A.B. Chaudhuri

Acknowledgement

The theme of this book developed as I was working on the problem of witch-killings among Santals. In this endeavour, I owe much to Dr.A.K.Das, Director, Cultural Research Institute, Government of West Bengal. In his infinite patience, and affection for me, Dr. Das helped me throughout the preparation of the book. Dr. Manas Kamal Chaudhuri of the C.R.I. helped me in analysing the collected data. Most of the songs composed by Jitu were collected and presented for this book by my friend Francis Hopna Hembram, a Santali poet living at Gopalpur in Banshihari Police Station, district West Dinajpur. Dr. Hitesh Ranjan Sanyal of the Centre for the Studies in Social Sciences, Calcutta favoured me with quite a few suggestions which evidently enhanced the worth of this work. I humbly acknowledge my debts to them, though the formal expressions of gratitude would never be adequate.

To my wife Sm. Bijayluxmi Chaudhuri I owe the continued assistance and support, as in everything.

With humility I present the book to the readers, owning all the inadequacies.

Prologue

Prologue

The aboriginal ethnic groups receded in the background as the Aryans advanced through conquest. The conquered helots found an insignificant role in the system to work hard to produce wealth of which they accrued little. Great discrimination ruled the society, and to sustain the discrimination reaping great economic advantages, the institutions of the King and the State came into being. Thus the King of a State came to be considered as the source of all power.

To the ethnic groups suffering on account of such discrimination, it appeared that those who ruled had grown selfish and their thoughts were evil. In their lust for power, they oppressed and persecuted others. They sowed the seeds of hatred. Through force or guile men and women were taught by those wicked rulers to debase themselves before their wealth and power. Homes were broken. The ethnic groups were weighed down by misery brought about by the depredations of power of the dominant Hindu society. The only way to redeem themselves from their plight was to seize power.The valiant and virile tribes braved the peril. In solidarity lay their strength.

For centuries, ethnic groups were being diffused in the Hindu society, either as Shudras or as Kshatriyas. The Shudras were necessary to help in the expansion of agriculture and productioin. Only when the dominant Hindu society encountered severe stress on account of extraneous alien forces or factors it allowed the induction of ethnic groups as Kshatriyas provided such ethnic groups retained their group solidarity backed by adequate economic strength arising out of stable agricultural societies. The reputation of military prowess was an added consideration. On the other hand, the idea of Kshatriyisation was inseparably linked with the urge of establishment of political power, or consolidation of political power attained, through investiture of prestige. The temporal success was to be blessed by the Brahmanas who obtained their share in the prosperity, and ever retained their social

The Chronicle

In the third decade of the twentieth century there took place an uprising of the Santals in Malda district in West Bengal. The uprising was quelled by the British Government by actual use of force. The incident found place in the official chronicle of the district-the District Handbooks-Malda-Census 1951 and the culmination of the movement was shown to have ended in the shoot-down that ended the life of Jitu Santal, the leader of the uprising. In reality, the incident had its impact on the administration to the extent of creating a new department for administering the welfare of the tribals. To contain the tribals, a new system of administration for the tribals along tribal line had to be introduced. The exploits of Jitu Sardar had reached the recesses of the tribal minds, and the sentiments have been spilling in new urges of tribal awakening, to find a way to better days. The movement of Jitu had been the culmination of a long series of movement along defensive stance starting from Bhagrit Baba in 1871 in the Santal Parganas. The tribal mind thereafter sought to assert its tribal entity, after a brief pause, leading to another revivalistic movement as we experience now-a-days in the Jharkhand and similar movement. An humble endeavour has been made in the following pages, along the lines of the chronicle, to bring out the salient features of the movement.

The chronicle runs thus:

"In character the Santals are naturally simple and straightforward, though contact with some of their less honest neighbours tend to make them suspicious and crafty. They are very superstitious and in some matters extremely credulous. The Satyam Shibam Sect, for example, was under the leadership of one Jitu Santal, whose wildest pronouncements were accepted by his followers as gospel truth. The Air Survey Company's aeroplane, when photographing over Habibpur thana, was reported to be an incarnation of Krishna. Another dictum of Jitu was that the payment of rent to landlords had been prohibited and the only payment required was a basketful of paddy to himself. As not infrequently happens with these movements the Satyam Shibam Sect tended to get mixed up with politics, and though it made no outward demonstration during the Civil Disobedience Movement of 1931, it was always a potential source of trouble. The culminating point came when Jitu and a number of his followers proclaimed their "Independence" and occupied the great mosque at Adina. Eventually an engagement took place in which one constable was killed by a poisoned arrow, Jitu was shot dead, and several other Santals were wounded. All this would never have taken place if the Santals were not so astonishingly credulous, and if Jitu's activities could have been limited. Unfortunately attempts to restrict his liberty did not find favour with the High Court.[1]

The chronicle outlines the incident deftly, but choses to remain silent on the aspiration of a tribe that was in quest of economic liberation from exploitation of a dominant society, to ensure prestige by asserting its tribal identity, to wrest for itself power so that it could build a permanent agricultural village society for itself. Nor does the chronicle dwell on the attempt to establish a state for the Santals by the Santals themselves and that the leader (who was shot dead) was a projection of the society engaged in class struggle for centuries. The nature of the place where this movement had developed was not indicated either. It was essentially a conclave, away from the main culture-centre of the Santals in the Santal Parganas, a thin flow of cultural continum trickling in through the preceptors of the Sapha Hor movement. The reference to the charisma of the leader has been made obliquely, and the 'unfortunate' lack of sympathy on the part of the Court to the attempts at restricting the activities of the leader has also been commented upon, signifying the mind of the general administration of the time.

In the following pages, the available evidence has been scanned to highlight the various facets of the movement which was not an isolated one but a bead in a string of pearls. Before embarking on the incident proper, let us discuss in brief the tribe, its social organisation and struggle for a foothold for centuries.

---

1. Mitra: District Handbooks—Malda Census 1951, P.XXII

Contents

Chapter 1

The Santals

The Santal is a large Proto-Australoid tribe found in West Bengal, northern Orissa, Bihar, Assam as also in Bangladesh. Linguistically they have been classified as Kolarians. According to Rev. Skrefsrud, Santal is a corruption of the word Saontar, and was given to the tribe because of their sojourn in the Saont or Samantabhumi (modern Silda Pargana of Midnapore district in West Bengal) for several generations. Suniti Kumar Chatterjee traces the word from Simanta + al—>Saontal. It is to be noted that the appelation has been given to the tribe by aliens; among themselves and their cognates, the term used is Ho or Horo or Hor, meaning 'man'. The Santal is one of the largest among tribes in India, numbering about 4 millions. A conscious attempt to establish a new identity in tribal reckoning is afoot. They have remarkable oral traditions and folk-lore, but no script. The solidarity having been broken, the Santals are gradually adopting languages of the areas inhabited, like Oriya in Orissa, Hindi in Bihar and Bengali in West Bengal and Bangladesh, thereby getting bi-lingual. It is one of the most discussed tribes in India. This distinction has been won by the tribe on account of the Santal Insurrection of 1855-56. Some claim the incident as the first national movement against the British government. Some feel that the honour of the first myrtirs should have been bestowed on Sido-Kanhu, the leaders of the movement, rather than on Mangal Pandey. For that matter, there are other claimants as well. While considering organised resistance to the British in India after their obtaining power, we may not ignore the 'rebellion' of Rangpur in 1773 and the subsequent struggle in which Md. Nuruluddin and Dayaram Seal, the Nabab and the Dewan respectively of the government established by the rebels, were killed in battle.[1] However, the aspirations of the

---

1. Das, Sukumar: Uttarbanger Itihas, pp.179-182

tribe in shaping itself as a permanent agricultural society were clear from the accounts of all earlier authorities.

It happened that the tribe had a different appellation in olden days—they were called Kharwars. The oral traditions speak of a series of migrations necessitated ostensibly to save the honour of their womenfolk. In this regard, the statement of Baghrai as noted by Dalton is interesting enough, though it did not preclude the possibility of projecting a myth to cover the inadequacies of a beaten social leadership. The Santals are considered to be inveterate imigrants. They are said to restrict their migration along the laterite soil. Their population is also fast increasing, and this pressure of population has caused the people to migrate far and wide. A steady growth of myths and lores about themselves and the surroundings reveals a positive reaction of the tribe to external stimuli.

The original abode of the tribe has been mentioned as Hihiri Pipiri whose exact identity is surrounded in mystery. Authorities differ on the exact location of the place. Some say that the Santals had come to the Indian Peninsula much before the Indo-Aryans, through Khyber and Bolan Passes under their leaders many of whom were deified as personal gods like Abge Bongas and Orak Bongas. The various theories on migration of the tribe are rather built up on the interpretations of the oral traditions of the tribe. Risley did not see it fit to attach undue credibility on these traditions, for, in his opinion, in the absence of bards or a written tradition, the chronological exactitude could not be maintained, nor the basic data would remain reliable. Risley took Hihiri Pipiri as Pargana Ahuri in the north-west of Hazaribag district in Bihar. Large settlements of Santals had been there at Chae and Champa Parganas of the same district. Tradition speaks of a Santal King named Jaura who destroyed himself and his family on hearing the approach of a Muhammadan army under Sayyid Ibrahim Ali alias Malik Bay, a general of Muhammad Tughlak, who died in 1353 A.D. The date of taking over the fort of Jaura if assumed in 1340 A.D., the subsequent migrations of the tribe as revealed in traditions would fill up the gap of time intervening between the departure of the tribe from Chae-Champa and their settlement in the present Santal Parganas. The earliest settlements like Hihiri Pipiri and Chae-Champa lie on the north-Western frontier of the table-land of Hazaribag and in the direct line of advance of the numerous Hindu immigrants from Bihar. The influx of the Hindus had actually driven out the Santals eastward and the line of retreat corresponds to that attributed in the legends.[2]

Suffice it to say that the tribe had lived for centuries in Chhotanagpur and the adjoining district which proved a sanctuary in which they lived almost in isolation until modern times. They have maintained a complete form of social organisation, based on the village and a union of villages. Its origin may be sought in the foundation of a village in the forest by a family or group of families connected by descent from a common ancestor in the male line. They cleared the jungle and brought the land under cultivation and held the land for the community jointly. A headman was elected, but the real control remained with the village council termed 'More Hor' (literally meaning the five persons) composed of the village elders. With the increase in population, new villages were set up, with their community leaders. As all these villages sprang up from blood relations, a form of connection was maintained which eventually developed into federations of villages. In such federations (Parganas) the organisation of the village was reproduced, excluding the religious functions. The basic unit is the village under Manjhi whose presence is necessary at all public functions. Should the village be under any headman of a different tribe, the Santals elect their headman for the discharge of religious and social functions and name him 'Handi Majhi' or liquor Manjhi. A hint of suborning the relilgious functionary in the society (Naeke) to the temporal leader in Manjhi would be clear from the election of the Handi Manjhi.The headman's powers are derived from the villagers, and he calls them together to discuss and decide on major questions of common interest as well as to try any one

2. Risley, H.H.: The Tribes and Castes of Bengal (Vol. I & II), 1891.

accused of a serious social offence. The More Hor is the exact parallel of the Indian term Panchayat similarity with the Vedic village organisations like Kulapati. Vispati and Janapadapati is discernible in the social organisations of the Santals. The village council meets at the council house-a simple shed in front of the deity Manjhi Haram representing the spirits of the founder of the village or the symbol of social leadership. "Although the offices of the headman and his colleagues are hereditary, the villagers have a meeting once a year at which after the performance of some sacrifices, the headman resigns his post to the people and his fellow officers follow suit. Their offices are formally given back by the people and resumed by them a few days later. The villagers, on the other hand, surrender their lands to the headman, using a form of words which means that they only retain their bodies and their wives. The lands are formally accepted by the Manjhi and formally given back"[3].

As we shall find later, surrender of land to the Manjhi could not perhaps take place in the Barind. The lands are ryotwari. Lands are given in usufructuary mortgage by improverished tribals. As such, even if the social function takes place, the handing over of land would be a matter of ritual only. Besides, individual allotment of land resorted to at a later stage of the permanent settlement had itself caused a flutter among the tribals, for, that was against the tribal rational. With the accrual of power and affluence-within the community-the Manjhies became stronger which ultimately reduced the annual custom of surrendering the post to a mere ritual formalilty. The same holds good in case of surrendering land by the villagers to the Manjhi.

No administrative job has been assigned to the Manjhi in Barind. Unlike the Manjhies in the Santal Parganas, he does not collect rents etc.; nor does he deal with the civil authorities direct. In the Barind, the Manjhi is not appointed by the Magistrate of the district. If a Manjhi dies, he is succeeded by

---

3. O'Malley, L.S.S.: India's Social Heritage, P.89

his heir if he is competent; or a new Manjhi may be elected by the villagers. Should the Manjhi be found guilty of gross a-social behaviour, the villagers may find a new one by election.

Villages are grouped in unions called Pargana with headman (Parganait) and his council in which the Manjhies of the included villages are there as also other persons of influence in the neighbourhood. This superior council decides matters too important to be disposed of by a village council and also adjudicates on appeals from its orders. There is another council-the highest among the Santala-which sits at the time of the annual hunt. This hunt is convened by the Dihri who is both master of the hunt and sacrificial priest. Hundreds of Santals take part in these hunt with arms and drive through the forest for three days killing every bird or beast they come across on the way. During such Disam Sendra, at the Lo Bir or Jungle Council, assembled tribals decide any matter brought before them and excommunicate grave offenders.

Apart from the temporal leadership of the Manjhi, there are other elected village officials like the Paranik (assistant to Manjhi), Jogmanjhi (guardian of morals), Naike (priest), Kudam Naike (assistant priest) and Godet (messenger). All these officials have specified roles to play within the village community. In many places, the roles of the Manjhi and the Naike have been rolled into the same man-the Manjhi.

Unlike the Hindu society, the Santals recognised the necessity of combining the temporal and spiritual leaderships in one individual at the apex. At the village, the Manjhi is the temporal leader. Though he has some religious functions to perform, viz. worship of the Manjhi Haram situated invariably opposite to his house, the religious functions of the community are conducted by the Naike and the Kudam Naike. In ritualistic matters, the Naike is independent of the Manjhi. Thus, the two strains of leadership in the vilage community is very clear. It may be mentioned in passing that individuals have their respective Abge Bongas and Orak Bongas (personal household gods) and the worship of these Bongas is done by the individuals severally and exclusively, such worship having no bearing on the societal leadership. The community gods are placed at the Jaher Than outside the village boundary and the Naike and his assistant perform religious rites on behalf of the village community there as well as in the village. In the Pargana, there is no religious functionary like the Naike or Kudam Naike. The Parganit has no religious duty either; his functions are administrative. That is true for his assistant the Desmanjhi as well. The temporal and the spiritual aspects of leadership converge in the Dihri who happens to be the Master of Hunts and the Sacrificial Priest rolled in one during Disam Sendra. It is thus clear that the Santals had provided for combining both the forms of leadership-temporal and spiritual on special occasions, signifying the acceptance of the idea of unity in command at the apex. Emergence of the charismatic leaders in the Santal community was always preceded by conditioning of the community, through myths and beliefs, to ideas favourable to forging a charismatic leader for some specific purpose. It is for a temporal cause that such leaders emerged in the Santal community and the manifestations were also on the mundane plane. The Santals found a term for such a charismatic leader-Subah Thakur, who may not come up from the traditional societal leadership always. While the Hindus evinced distinct disinclination in allowing the merger of these two forms of leadership in one individual, the Santals availed of the process several times in a bid to obtain political power. It may be recalled that the Basudeva cult could not thrive among the Hindus, and in the Hindu social stratification, the king and the priest are separate entities. In Hindus reckoning, the spiritual had always an edge over the temporal, and that eventually led to Brahmanical superiority in the society, as the Brahmanas came to control the access to prestige. But the social stratification of the Santal society are not that complex either.

The legend of dispersal of the tribe starts from Hihiri Pipiri due to increase in population. The Santals went to Harataburu where the entire tribe but a couple was destroyed by the Jug Sengel (a tornado of fire that razed for seven days at the bidding of Thakur-the Supreme Deity). From the surviving couple, the tribe sprang up once again. From Hora, the tribe went to Sasangbera, a plain on the bank of a great river. According to Kolean Guru, the Parish divisions were made at Sasangbera. Therefrom they went to Jarpi where they encountered the Great Mountain (Marang Buru) through which they could not find a pass. Only after paying homage to the Great Mountain the tribe found a pass leading to Ahiri. They stayed there for some time and crossed over to Kendi, Chae and finally Champa. In Champa they lived for several generations and the present social institutions were evolved. In reorganising the society, the Santals leaned heavily on the condign power, as a poor society can hardly afford to take recourse to the compensatory power, particularly on the mundane plane. Social conditioning continued through lores and legends and myths developed on the social values to be respected, or ideas to be shunned. At Champa, the tribe built up 'garhs' or forts, to protect themselves from enemies. Khairigarh was held by the Hembrans, Koindagarh by Kiskus; Champagarh belonged to the Murmus, Badligarh held by Mandis, Simgarh belonged to the Tudus. There were many other garhs whose names Kolean could not recollect. It is from Champa that shibboleths of the tribe developed. Kolean also maintained that Marang Buru, Moreiko Turuiko and Jaher Era were set up at Jaher Than while the tribe was at Champa[4]. At last the Hindus drove them out of Champa, and they established themselves at Saont where they lived for about two hundred years. Again pressed by the Hindus, they wandered to the eastern part of Manbhum near Panchet under Raja Hambir Singh. Here the Raja adopted Hindu religion and set up himself as Rajput. But the people did not like to change their religion, and forsook the King and wandered off to what is called the Santal Parganas presently.

The ostensible reasons of migration expressed in the legends of the tribe appear to be designed to conceal the failures of the tribal leadership in securing and adhering to a firmbase for the tribe. The tribe was keen to establish itself as

---

4. Hansda, Baidyanath (Trans): Marc Hapramko Reak Katha.

a permanent agricultural village society, but could not achieve the same on account of numerous Hindu immigrants dislodging it time and again from earlier days even. It is certain that the Santals were losing land to the Hindus in Saont as well. Along with the loss of land, Hindu acculturation was a positive threat to the tribe as would be evident from the introduction of the tattoo marks on women and 'sika'-marks on the menfolk, to highlight their group identity. The strain on the social solidarity led to more rigorous measures of social control. It was, however, not so much for the threat of social disintegration by way of Hindu acculturation as for the loss of land affecting the sustenance of the tribe that the migration from Saont took place. The same reason was at the back of the migration from Shikhar. The Santal legends say that the King having embraced Hinduism, the Santals left Shikhar. This fact was not the whole truth either. Behind the legend, the failure of the tribe and its leadership in adjusting themselves to a changed system of land-revenue administration in Shikhar which took to the money-economy instead of continuing to accept taxes in kind, is palpable. It may be recalled that King Durjanshal had been taken captive to Delhi where he saw the splendour of the royal courts and the associated pomp. Back in his kingdom, he wanted to have a palace befitting the dignity of the King by the new reckoning. Previously he was living in a mud-house, spacious though. Now, to defray the expenses, he had to lean on the cash instead of the kind; the land-revenue system, and the land-distribution in consequence, underwent a drastic change. To run the changed pattern of administration, the King had to induct Hindus who were adept in the system. Induction included Brahmanas who added prestige to the King and the royal family by innovating Kshatriya genealogical tables, and giving validity to the Kshatriya claim of the royal household.

The services rendered were certainly not without price; the Hindus (including the Brahmanas) were given land-grants to sustain themselves as also to support the King. The exactions by the tax collectors were many times the demand of the royal court and in consequence, the money-lender entered the field.

Kolean lamented that since the days of Shikhar, the money-lender did not leave the tribe in peace. In the bargain, the Santals lost their land and migrated to the Santal Parganas. It may be noted that the tribe had similar experiences there as well.

The Santals cleared land and started cultivation in their new habitat. Soon the simple tribals fell prey to the wily money-lenders and landlords. They were being steadily deprived of their possessions, leading them to a stage of perpetual bondage to the creditors. No redress was effected by the administration. The seething discontent broke in a revolt in 1855-56. Thousands perished. The Santal Parganas came into being in 1855 with a simple form of administration. But the Rent Act of 1859 and the Civil Procedure Code of the same year enabled the money-lender and the landlords to grip the Santals with renewed vigour. The Santals became restive and in 1871, assembled in tumultuous gatherings which ultimately convinced the administration of the necessity of allaying the resentment by suitable enactments. A regulation was passed in 1872 debarring exhorbitant interest on loans, sanctioning a record of rights of the landlords and the tenants, and authorising the government to exclude laws unsuitable to the Santal Parganas from implementation. But the drought in the following years compelled people to migrate from Damin-i-koh. The famine took a great toll. It is during this period after 1871 that Santals crossed over the Ganges across Rajmahal and entered into Barind. Crossing the Ganges at Rajmahal by some tribals has been mentioned by Kolean Guru in his accounts. It is said that a few families had crossed over the Ganges in 1855-56 to avoid the involvement in the insurrection, but no official document could be gathered to prove this point conclusively. According to this unconfirmed report, two groups of Santals had arrived-one at Pakuahat in Bamangola thana in Malda district, and the other at Hili (presently in West Dinajpur District).

Around 1871, the local landlords of Malda and Dinajpur inducted Santals to break the land full of jungle, for cultivation.The census of 1872 revealed a Santal population of 215 in

Malda district. By 1818, the number of Santals in Malda swelled up to 1734. This must have been due to migration of families from other districts, as would be evident from a study of the census figures. While Santal population increased in Burdwan, Dinajpur, Bogra, Pabna, Darjeeling, Singbhum and some tributary states, notably Mayurbhanj, population decreased perceptibly in Bankura, Birbhum, Midnapore, Murshidabad, Monghyr, Bhagalpore and Santal Parganas. The migration had started for hunger; the dispersal was almost in every direction,. It is at this stage that Santals in great numbers were taken to Assam to work in the tea gardens. Gradually, this dispersal of the tribe spread over the wide geographical area as is inhabited by the Santals presently. But these migrations did not affect the solidarity of the tribe to any remarkable extent. The internal control and corresponding submission to such control helped the tribe in maintaining its defensive shell. Santals in Santal Parganas had re-created the tribal atmosphere of society, and later carried those ideas to wherever they went. It was, however, impaired in the industrial set up. As Martin Orans observes, "Thus it is not simply migration which is responsible for diminished solidarity, but migration to industrial set up."[5]

It may be mentioned in passing that the Santals and its cognates had been living generally in the area beyond the Madhyadesa of the Brahmanical concept, where they had taken refuge in the jungles. The extension of the agricultural economy in the eastern direction after the Gupta period had pushed them farther in the jungles. The forests were being systematically denuded to bring more land under cultivation and ultimately, these tribals had to succumb to the pressures and themselves came out to partake of the developing economy, for sustenance. By the time the permanent settlement was clamped on Bengal, the Santals had attuned themselves to clearing the forest and bring the land under cultivation. This developed faculty had led to their migration to various places

5. Orans, Martin (1965): The Santal: A Tribe in Search of Great Traditions, p. 81

for agricultural operations. Along with had started a renewed search for a permanent foothold. Thus, the Santals came in closer contact with the alien Hindu culture out of economic necessity.

Like so many tribes, the Santals have been living in close proximity with the Hindus, retaining the core of their tribal identity against odds, and progressing. The aspiration of the tribe to settle down as a permanent agricultural society has not yet been fulfilled, and the struggle has been continuing. According to Mare Hapramko Reak Katha, all the aborigines had accompanied Ramchandra to Lanka and fought for him; that is why-for a long time, there was no clash between the tribals and the 'Dekos'.

The Hindus lived in the plains and the tribes lived in the hills and jungles. Kolean also mentioned the problem of land alienation-Hindus snatching away land whenever it was cleared by the tribals[6]. In fact, the very word Deko carries the memory of the distant past, when with the spread of Sanskritisation, the Deva or Brahmana would come down to the land of the aborigines and would settle down there. This practice subsequently gave way to another practice of granting land endowments to Brahmanas, in tribal areas from the Gupta period onwards, even by converted Kshatriyas.

Historical evidence of granting land-endowments to Brahmanas are available in plenty. Arthasastra is explicit in enunciating the principle mentioning the Brahmanas specifically who were eligible to accept Brahmadeyas, free of rent and taxes. Mention is made of various officials who should be granted land. The matter does not end there. Out of the land not fit for cultivation, the King would create pasture; he would create Brahmaranya where learned Brahmanas could read Vedas, and Somaranya bearing trees fit for use in Soma sacrifices, and donate those to the Brahmanas. Likewise, the King would donate land to the hermits out of such land[7].

---

6. Mare Hapramko Reak Katha : p. 5.
7. Basak, R.: Kautiliya Arthasastra (Vol.I) Pp 27-28 (Janapadanibesha and Bhumichchidra Prakaranas)

With the expansion of the agricultural economy, more and more 'janapadas' were being created. The grant of land to the Brahmanas resulted in the establishment of Brahmanical nuclei in the new areas leading to Sanskritic acculturation. Penetration of the Brahmanas in the tribal belts added enormously to the number of Shudras. At the same time, the King's mandate at once alienated the inherent right of the peasant on the land cultivated so long by him. The peasant came to have an overlord. "Except Tamilnadu and Kerala, it was in the fifth- seventh centuries that large-scale land grants came to be made to the Brahmanas in the peripheral areas such as Assam, Bengal, Orissa, Central India, Gujarat and the Deccan, and also in the Himalayan areas and Nepal"[8]. Brahmana land-holdings increased in number through Brahmadeyas and Agrahara grants. In the Gupta period an office of Agraharika was created presumably to keep records of such grants.

Irfan Habib traces the process in the growth in the power and pretensions of the ruler or chief (Rajan, Kshatriya) thus:"In the beginning his claim seems to have been over a 16th of the produce of the land; and he also aspired to an undefined share 'in villages, in horses, in kine.' Afterwards he levied a tax, bali, of an undefined nature, from the vaisyas, or peasants. Furthermore, he began to grant authority over lands and villages to his lesser chiefs (Kshatriyas). Finally, we see him giving away lands and villages to Brahamanas. Such grants were apparently first made with the consent of the vis, or the peasant community, but in course of time the grants tended to become arbitrary acts of the King, and as such appear to have aroused some protest[9]. These new land-holders reaped the benefit of the cleared land which eventually paved the way of feudalism with the transfer of all sources of revenue and surrender of police and administrative functions. The word 'Deko' was obtained by accepting the word 'Deva' in the Santali, naturalising

8. Sharma, R.S.: 'Material Milieu of Tantricism' in 'Indian Society; Historical Probings' p. 178

9. Habib, Irfan: 'Landed Property in Pre-British India' in 'Indian Society: Historial Probings', p. 270

it and adding suffix of 'ko' indicating plurality (Deva + Ko = Devako - Deoko - Deko/Diku)[10]. The association of deprivation with this word finds ample expression in the tribal's manner. Currently a new dimension is being added to the concept of Deko in that tribals getting rich by exploiting tribals are also referred to in the same vain. The sentiment associated with the word Deko is much more intense, deep-seated than the probable reaction to persons annoying the tribals (expressed in terms'dik dik karnewale' or like). 'Dik' is too mild a term for deprivation and the associated sentiment involves not only the Brahamanas but all the outsiders who appear to have acquired property. It may be noticed that the Santals do not have similar distaste for the Kamar or other depressed classes in as much as they did not happen to be associated with the deprivation of the landed property. One may tend to disagree with Ranajit Guha in his etymological interpretation of the word diku[11]. The antagonism implied in the term is directed against the high castes forming an economic stratum, and the ethnic identity merged with the class identity of the tribals gets accentuated during periods of strain or stress.[12]

10. I am grateful to my friend G.C. Murmu of Indian Police Service for first suggesting such a derivation of the word on philological considerations.
11. Guha, Ranajit: Elementary Aspects of Peasant Insurgency in Colonial India, p. 281
12. Sinha, S.C.; Sen, J; Panchbhai.S.:'The Concept of Diku Among the Tribes of Chotanagpur', Man in India (Vol. 49-No. 2).

Chapter 2

Interactions

With the development of stable agricultural societies with food surpluses started the continuous and extensive contact among members of different societies. This led to the development of larger political groups and multigroup societies, through conquest and migration.

Social life is characterised by reciprocal expectations to a large extent.

Like any other society with permanent stratifications – the Hindu social stratifications had the following elements working underneath: (i) control over economic goods and services, (ii) control over social honour, and (iii) control over the activities of other persons. These elements are closely related, but not identical. The situation tends to be different when these elements get separated. Persons without prestige or power may find themselves with high income; or persons without income or prestige may find themselves with power. In the same circumstances, some of those who formerly possessed income, prestige and power may find one or more of these values fading - the basis of their power swept away by social changes. The more the pressure on the society, the more 'closed' it gets - a prelude to a defensive stance. It corresponds with a loss in the attributes, particularly power and prestige.

Stratification is the basic organisational feature of societies. Differentiation precedes stratification and then accompanies it. The rewards of the society are distributed unequally and the inequality is instilled in the social structure so that it persists through generations. In that context, the attitude of the less powerful ethnic groups may find expression in the manner suggested by Lewis Wirth in assimilation, pluralism, secession and domination. The primary theme has been spelled out by Prof. Milton Yinger thus : Let us disappear as a group, judge us as only individuals–assimilation; let us maintain our group identity, based perhaps on language, race, religion or culture, so long as we give full allegiance to society - pluralism; give us our freedom, let us establish our own society where we can practise our way of life without hindrance - secession; we are weary of being dominated, and we shall do everything we can to reverse the present status arrangement, by militant means, if necessary - domination."[1]

Perpetuation of discrimination is effected where there are great economic and other advantages to be derived. This unjust continuation of discrimination is normally held up by developing a comforting rationalisation: the minority is a lying, thieving, murdering savage. This rationalisation gets embedded in the culture so that the idea persists and socialisation proceeds in that line. The insecurity of the dominant group, and individuals having inadequate socialisation, tend to make them more aggressive to the minority to render the rancour and splean in them expressed in terms of justice and social cause-for, the minority is powerless. The rationalisation breeds its justification, by creating adverse circumstances for the minority group. Many of them become cruel, lacking ambition, untrustworthy. They learn self-hatred, to lack motivation, to feel less than fully attached to the society which maltreats them so. Some of them fight. All these again go to prove the rationalisation of the dominant group.

When the members of a group see no way out of their difficulties, when they feel utterly helpless, they are liable to accept symbolic schemes that promise them relief and a sense of meaning. They become true believers. This is why the Santals are 'astonishingly credulour'. Also to negate the derogatory ideas of the dominant groups, the minority groups may initiate movements to lift the members up towards the customs of the dominant society by emulating them, as happened with the Sapha Hor movement and the Satyam Shibam sect. These sects imparted moral tenets and observances along Hindu ideals like purificatory bath, fast, etc.

---

1. Yinger, Milton J. (1965): A Minority Group in American Society.

The caste system in India arose out of economic factors. The dominant groups held sway over others on the relative strength accrued out of economic activities and sought to develop a self-sufficient village community wherein they controlled the entry of other ethnic groups who had reached the periphery of the village community. The Brahmanas had the sway in the society. The Brahmanical power over the society was drastically cut short during the rule of the Mauryas and in this period, several tribes had been inducted in the Hindu society as Kshatriyas. It may be recalled that the Maurya dynasty was Shudra in origin. Asoka's appointment of 'Dharma Mahamatras' and the precept of 'Ahimsa' had dealt severe blows on the Brahmanical rights and privileges so long enjoyed, and the principles of 'Danda Samata' (equality of punishment) and Vyavahara Samata (equality in law suits) made the people of the empire equal in the eyes of the law irrespective of caste, creed or colour. The Puranas tell us of a valiant King Visvasphani or Visvasphatik who would make Kings out of the untouchable and degraded classes like Kaibartas, Panchakas and Pulindas. By overthrowing the ruling Kshatriya caste, he created a new Kshatriya caste. This might indicate that the old ruling nobility was destroyed and a new ruling class was created. Pargiter fixed this period around 300 B.C. and that leads us to the supposition that Visvasphani might be Mahapadma Nanda.[2] The social tenets of Arthasastra of Kautilya were reversed by the Manava Dharmasastra or Manusmriti during the Sunga period which heralded a Brahmanical revival. Pushyamitra usurped the throne by murdering the last Nanda King Brihadratha in 184 B.C. Manusmriti was accepted by the Hindu society of the Madhyadesa (of the Brahmanical concept) and the eastern region. The rigours of the Shastric injunctions were imposed once again. As the Hindus gradually lost their foreign trade after the fall of the Imperial Guptas, development of an agricultural economy in the country, particularly in the northern and eastern regions was found necessary. The tribals were not allowed to come as

---

2. Datta, Bhupendranath (1983): Studies in Indian Social Polity.

close as in the times of the Mauryas. Same were, however, allowed to come and participate in the developing agricultural economy or in the ancillary trades in a very limited way, and given a place in the lowest stratum of the Hindu society as Shudras. The royal power and the Hindu society were almost indivisible, and the former as a rule did not stand against the mandates of the latter.

It is not always that all members of an assimilated tribal group were given the same place in the Brahmanical order. "Finding the mention of 'Nisadagotra' in the Ganapatha of Panini, Kosambi suggested that some Brahmanas had either been adopted from the aboriginal priests or had served the aborigines as priests. The role of the Brahmana as an instrument of raising social status has not been questioned in any way. It may be that the large majority of the Nisadas remained backward and uninducted, and this might have prompted the lawgivers to place the caste at the lowest anuloma level."[3] Nor did all the assimilated groups find the same place in the caste hierarchy. Depending on economic power obtained and group solidarity retained, such groups were placed in the caste hierarchy mostly as Shudras but some as Kshatriyas.

Question may arise as to why the tribals were keen to join the Hindu social structure even after so-called tyranny of the caste Hindus. We have already mentioned the economic compulsions of the ethnic groups. As they came gradually to the proximity of the Hindu village, gradual acculturation led to exchange of ideas and customs. The ethnic groups were allowed by and large to follow their own beliefs and in many cases, rituals if those did not go beyond the Hindu acceptance absolutely. This freedom enjoyed by the ethnic groups allowed the retention of the culture-traces of such groups even though they were accepted with the Hindu social stratification. This freedom was not possible in case of conversion to Islam.

---

3. Jha. V: 'From Tribe to Untouchable: The Case of Nisadas' in Indian Society: Historical Probings, pp. 71-72.

The ethnic groups were also allowed to worship their own gods. The phenomenal rise in the number of Hindu gods/deities can be attributed to this feature. An examination of the Hindu pantheon will prove the inclusion of local gods/deities in numbers, apart from the elemental gods.

Through marriage also the various stratum came closer. The upward mobility initiated by a group of persons in any groups resulted in the upward mobility of the whole group. That is why, ethnic groups in the Pancham Varna were accommodated time and again in the Kshatriya category of the Hindu Varnasrama when they succeeded themselves in establishing as permanent agricultural village commmunities with a marked group solidarity. As the prevailing economic system had been agrarian, so due stress was given on being successful agriculturists.

Situation underwent drastic change after the arrival of the Muslims in the scene. It was felt necessary to build up a resilience in the Hindu society against the onslaught as the society was threatened with disintegration. Conversion was facilitated by the Buddhists smarting under the Brahmanical tyranny. Tribals with varying degrees of acculturation had also been watching from a distance. Some of the, notable the Santals, felt the impact of the onslaught of the Muslims-we may recall King Jaura of the Santali legend on this score. The tribals had an affinity with the Hindus whom they had been seeing for long. There were cultural exchanges too. They felt nearer to the Hindus. As the Hindus were controlling all the avenues of economic operations, the tribals had the incentive, and they acknowledged the superiority of the upper caste Hindus and joined the society as subordinate allies. The expanding agricultural system needed the sinews and muscles of the aborigines. It may also be seen that the earlier invaders were also absorbed in the Hindu society in a similar fashion. The Rajputs are enough illustrations of the process, who were inducted after sacrifical performances according to the Hindu rites. Agnikula Rajputs and similar ethnic groups had become dominant by acquiring economic and political power; hereby they acquired prestige as well. In case of necessity, myths were created and ethnic groups were associated with those myths to favour induction. When pressure from exogenous sources like Muslim invaders got too strong, the Hindu society grew defensive. Manu and Patanjali classed the Sakas and the Yavanas as Shudras and placed them above the so-called untouchable 'varnas'; but the bearded, horse-riding, beef-eating Turuskas (Turks) were mentioned as one group of Mlechchhas and their touch was regarded as more polluting than the Chandala as we find in the difference of penances ordained in both the texts. Though the formulated injunctions appear to be later interpolations, it is evident that these were formulated at a period when the Turks came to be known to the Hindus and the struggle with the Central Asian Hordes had been intense.

The intrusion of Islam in India was unlike the invasion of the ancient times. The individual Yavanas, the Sakas, the Kushans, the Huns could be assimilated in the Hindu society when they accepted some form of Hinduism and were completely Indianised. Along with a foreign religion, Islam brought in an alien civilization, rival to the Indian one in every respect. The converts had to change themselves completely in every way and they had to break away completely from the Indian traditions. Moreover, the international outlook of Islam was incompatible with Hindu orthodoxy. In consequence Hinduism in all its branches fell back on racial nationalism for self-preservation. Any compromise with Islam was taboo. This naturally led to all sorts of prohibitions which not only declared the new foreigners as Mlechchhas, but forbade any social contact with them. This attitude of the Hindus developed with the political struggle with the Muhammadans. The defeat and the threat of extinction caused by conversion to the rival religion and the breaking away from the old Indian ties by the converted Indians embittered the Hindus who not only tabooed all foreign contacts, but to prevent the members of the society from falling off the prescribed injunctions, the Hindu society became ossified and immobile. It encrusted itself and became static. Simultaneously, Hindu society relented on restrictions and rituals so far as variations of the Hindu religious observances and sects were concerned; the society accepted the outburst of the Bhakti cult and other variants. Subsequently, Hindus came round through reformation movement of Shri Chaitanya and others through Bhakti cult, and stopped the erosion from the society. Tantricism also helped the Hindus on that score. A conscious attempt was made by the society to enlarge its base by inducting the aborigines in the Hindu fold. The writing of the Kalika Puranam in the twelth century is not without its significance. The conversion of various ethnic groups in the second decade of the twentieth century was the continuation of this intention.

When the political power slipped into the hands of the British, the Hindu society was in such quandary. With the stabilisation of the British rule, the Hindus again reacted to the fear of the apprehended Muslim preponderance. Partha Chatterjee traced the relation leading to accentuated tension between the two communities in Bengal to the modes of interests on land. A "perception about the agrarian structure of those districts [eastern and northern]- a predominantly Hindu land-owning class, a predominantly Muslim tenantry-the simple structural explanation of organised communal politics in Bengal came to be formulated with obvious clarity: the dominant upper caste Hindu Bhadralok, politically organized under the Congress, sought to protect and preserve the rights and privileges of the zamindari and intermediate tenure holding rentier interests, whereas Muslim leaders of eastern Bengal relying on the support of Muslim praja, sought to uphold the rights of raiyat and found themselves in opposition to the Congress. This was the basic structural foundation of the 'communal' divide in organized politics in Bengal, and the experience of the Tenancy Act debate of 1928, which dramatically brought this to the surface, appears to have finally convinced the new Muslim leadership of eastern Bengal of the need for independent political organisation. 'Neither in terms of the Muslim interest', writes Abul Mansur Ahmed, a Congress- Khilafatist who later played a crucial role in both the

Krishak Praja Party and the Muslim League, 'nor of the praja interest, was it possible any longer to rely on the Congress.'[4] With the growth of the nationalist movement, the British government in India had been feeling ill at ease. The Two-Nations theory propounded by Md. Ali Jinnah had stirred the emotion of the Hindus as well who felt the presence of the contender for political power. And this was the time when the Hindus decided to enlarge their base by inducting those ethnic groups living in the proximity. To facilitate the induction, the authority of the Kalika Puranam (Slokas 86:30-31) was invoked wherein it has been stated that for fear of Parashu Rama the Kshatriyas had been hiding in out of the way places not divulging their Kshatriya origin. On the authority of the Purana the Kshatriya attributes were invested on the ethnic groups, with the additional prospect of placemant high in the Chaturbarnya society. Thus the Rajbanshies (Bratya Kshatriyas) of North Bengal and the Hajangs (Gupta Kshatriyas) of Mymensingh were inducted in Hindu society as Kshatriyas, in the second decade of the twentieth century. These new entrants in the fold were allowed to wear the sacred thread, which privilege was till then being enjoyed by the Brahmanas. Taking on sacred thread as a token of being Kshatriya was noticed in other ethnic groups as well. In 1921, some Polis of village Dalla in Habibpur thana had taken on sacred thread which had led to intense excitement in the Poli Community there. In Chittagong and Mymensingh districts, the Hadis were also urged by political agitators to put on threads as Kshatriyas as also to get the fact recorded in zaminadari records.

While the sloka from Kalika Puranam admirably sufficed in case of the Rajbanshies, a new myth had to be created for the Hajangs. The Hindu Mission had published a pamphlet in 1927, claiming the Hajang as one of the lost Kshatriya tribes in oblivion since the days of Parashu Rama.

---

4. Chatterjee Partha:"Agrarian Relations and Communalism, 1926-35" in Subaltern Studies I (Ranajit Guha edited), p. 10.

Introducing the Hajangs, the pamphlet said that a group of people living in Mymensingh, Sylhet and the hill-regions of Assam claim themselves as Gupta Kshatriyas. When these people settled down at the above places, their neighbours the Garos called them Hajang, observing their great aptitude in agriculture. In Garo Language, 'ha'means earth, and 'jang' stands for worms. The history of this community is to be found in manuscripts retained at villages Kalikabari, Ghilagora in the Susang Pargana. The history runs as follows:-

King Pushparaksha of the Solar dynasty reigned at village Avanti. His son Pradaksha married Swarupa, daughter of King Kharva of the Lunar dynasty. King Pushparaksha was a devotee of Goddess Lakshmi. He was in possession of an amulet given to him by his deity. As long as the amulet was with him, Parashu Rama could not vanquish him in war. Thereafter, Parashu Rama stole the amulet in the guise of a Sanyasi (mendicant). In the war that followed, both Pushparaksha and his son were killed. Swarupa was carrying at that time. She took shelter in the hermitage of sage Kamadatta in the forest. The sage came to know of the situation in meditation and allowed the princess to stay at the hermitage. In due course, a son was born to Swarupa and he was called Pradangshu. With extreme devotion, Swarupa used to worship Goddess Kamakashya, the deity of sage Kamadatta, and had the boon from her that her descendants would continue to have the privilege of worshipping Goddess Kamakshya for ever. When Pradangshu grew up, his mother sought the advice of the sage about the ritual of taking up the sacred thread as a Kshatriya, whereupon she was advised to desist from that. Neither the sage nor the mother divulged the parentage of the son, out of fear. As such, the son did not know that he was the scion of a Kshatriya family.. In course of time, Pradangshu married Suthama, daughter of Kamadatta. Shortly thereafter, both Kamadatta and Swarupa died, so the ancestory of Pradangsdhu could not be disclosed. The Hajangs happen to be the descendants of Pradangshu and Suthama. As the Kshatriya identity of their ancestors was kept concealed, they are known as Gupta Kshatriyas.

From times immemorial, these people observe commensal obsequies on the thirteenth day like Kshatriyas. They maintain commensality with Brahamanas and Kayasthas and employ only Brahmanas for ritualistic performances. The community is divided in two sects: one is Baisnav (devotees of Hari) and the other is Shakta (devotees of Shakti). Their religious observances and rituals will find approval with the Hindu religious scriptures.

The pamphlet urged the Hindu Society in general to accept the Hajangs in the Hindu fold in response to their keenness to improve their status as a whole. That the simple yet powerful community is Hindu, there should be no doubt. Once inducted as Hindus, there is strong potentiality of the Community to develop into a pilllar of the Hindu Society.

It is curious to note that both the ethnic groups thus inducted had by that time established themselves as permanent agricultural village communities. They had also retained their group solidarity. It is evident that these communities availed of the agricultural ladder to gain access in the social hierarchy of the Hindus. The veering away of the Mahatos from the Santals on ostensible grounds of superiority and actual grounds of having developed a permanent agricultural base, is another instance of detribalisation.

Firm agricultural base coupled with military prowess had enabled some ethnic groups to elevate themselves to the Kshatriya status within the Hindu varnasrama. After such elevation and setting up of kingdoms, such ethnic groups arranged to have suitable genealogies to highlight their ancestry. As mentioned earlier, for such elevation, and for lending credibility to the genealogies, Brahmanas were inducted in large number within such tribal kingdoms by granting them land endowments and other allurements. K. Suresh Singh observes:

Following the decline of the Gupta empire, the wide eastern tract extending from the Himalayan foot hills to the Vindhya mountains witnessed the emergence of the rural foci of political power, led by autochthonous chieftains who acted as champions of neo-brahmanism. Doms, Bhars and Cheros in South Bihar, Kharwars in the Sone-Damodar Valley, Gonds and Rakshels in the Chattisgarh region and the Bhumij in the Jungle Mahals of Bengal filled the vacuum in the countryside in the medieval period...........Initial anti-brahamanism gave way to their support for brahmanism. They were elevated to the rank of Kshatriyas. The acculturated groups were then called Rajbhars, Rajgonds and Chavanbansi Cheros. The Hinduisation of tribes in Chhotanagpur or Jharkhand followed, and also the Tharus. Emergence of autochthons as kingdom- builders may be noticed among Ahoms (1228-1819) in Upper Assam, by the Gonds in Central India (15th to 18th centuries), by the Nagbanshies in Chhotanagpur and by the Cheros in South Bihar (Sahabad and Palamau). Kharwar jagirdars were serving under the Chero kings. They participated in the Palamau uprising in 1817 against the East India Company. The Chero kingdom had been away for arrear revenue in 1815. In the uprising of 1832 which was more broad-based the Chero and Kharwar jagirdars and their raiyats rose against the Company, partly against steep increase in revenue demand and partly for selling away the properties of jagirdars and the under-tenure holders for arrear of revenue. The bulk of Chero army was comprised of Chero and Kharwar warriors. The archers were recruited from every Chero and Kharwar family."[5]

With the change of time, particularly during the British regime, the Hindus lost the absolute śway over the economic field; they had not the power to prevent others in joining the economic field, as the power had been separated from them, the royal power having assumed a secular attitude.

With the power of the Hindu society declining, various ethnic groups felt less secure and less inclined to associate themselves with the old caste system. The incentive was not there. And with the compilation of the list of Scheduled Castes and Scheduled Tribes, and investing of additional rights by

5. Singh, K. Suresh: 'A Study in State Formation among Tribal Communities in Indian Society: Historical Probings.'

way of reservations, a conscious attempt to express their tribal or ethnic identity was discernible. The somewhat powerful ones sought to ensure the continuanace of the special rights, while some took to the revivalistic pattern of movements, preferring claims for independent principalities. These tribes or ethnic groups highlighted their differences from others, notably from the Hindus and have since been demanding autonomous powers for themselves. The objective is to secure political power which would bring economic power in its train. Suffice it to say that a drastic change in the attitude of some ethnic groups has been discernible, who have been citing intances of economic disparity-imaginary or real. The real quest is for political power. Dr. Surajit Sinha had also observed the phenomenon of the thought of re-tribalisation entering the mind of the aryanised tribes.[6]

Apart from the larger ethnic groups, some smaller groups have also caught the contagion. They have been asserting their particular ethnic identity in a bid to obtain concessions. We may take the case of the Kharwars of Malda. The group was listed as Scheduled Tribe in West Bengal in respect of Purulia District and the territories transferred from Purnea District of Bihar, and not elsewhere. A prosperous agricultural community, engaged as traders and professionals, having a firm agricultural base, this group had nothing to distinguish themselves apart from the Hindus. The titles that they had adopted were akin to the Hindus as well. Now, this community demanded that they be treated as Scheduled Tribe and did not hesitate to aproach the Hon'ble High Court when the administration expressed doubt about their contention. The zonal restriction having been withdrawn in 1977, the Kharwars of Malda were accepted as a Scheduled Tribe. Doubtless, the affluent Kharwars of Malda would make better use of the concessions available, as they are already ahead of many other tribes and castes in terms of affluence and education.

---

6. Sinha, S.C.: State Formation and Rajput Myth in Tribal Central India, in Man in India, vol.42, No.1, pp. 35-80.

It is to be observed that the process of re-tribalisation is gaining ground in the country. The Laskar Community in Tripura is yet another illustration. While the community has been enjoying the benefits of the upper class, the prospects of being thrown out of the schedule has reacted strongly. Long and protracted litigation over the issue between the community leaders and the Government of Tripura has been raging. The origin of the Laskars was due to a union of the tribals with immigrant Hindus. The members of the community had all along been in high positions in the royal service. As everywhere else, a group of affluent elites of the community has been conducting the movement.

Incidentally, it may be recalled that the Santals claimed relationship with the Kharwars at one time. This contention of Kolean Guru finds support in the statement of Bagh Rai as recorded by Dalton in his Descriptive Ethnology of Bengal. Dalton had developed that impression even before he had met Bagh Rai, and this impression of Dalton was supported by Mr. Mann and Mr. Hunter from their independent observations. Dalton writes, "In the traditions of Bihar and Sahabad, as given in Buchanon Hamilton's work, the Cheros, Kols and Kharwars are blended together, and it is probable that the Santals are not wrong in claiming relationship with the Kharwars, but by their own account the Santals have never played a prominent role in history; always clinging to the skirts of hills and forests and constantly shifting, they appear never to have advanced beyond the polity of a village community. Ignoring all relationship with other Kolarians, they yet have no tradition that they ever formed a nation or had a Raja or ruler of their own, and though great vocalists and melodists, they have no song commemorative of ancient glory. When they rose in 1855 A.D., it is probable that they contemplated no more than the extermination of their tormentors, the money-lenders. It is at all events the first time we hear of them in revolt, though so constantly migrating to avoid oppression. I cannot but think that the Mundas and Hos, who tenaciously cling to their holdings and have always shown themselves ready to fight for them, if necessary, must have the prestige of superior birth.

There are many reasons for supposing that the Cheros, who were a ruling race, and the Mudas and Hos, are of the same stock, but the Santals and Kharwars may have become one people with them after having been subjugated.

The Santals, like the Kharwars belong to, or have mixed much with, the dark races of India. The Cheros, Hos and Mundas are, on the whole, fairer and preserve more distinctly traits of the Tarter type."[7]

In 'Reak Katha' Kolean wondered when the Santals ceased to be known as Kharwars. On this score, the following observation of Dr. S.C. Sinha would be of interest:-

"Tribals at the lower rungs of social hierarchy were only feebly touched by the aspiration for identification as Rajput-Kshatriyas. Their poor economic condition, more than any other factor, virtually ruled out the possibility of ever realising the status of Rajput for which it is essestial to 'purchase' the ritual service' of brahmans of the right kind."[8] The Kharwars had lifted themselves up towards Hinduisation in close association with the Cheros and formed a part of the Chero army. The lower stratum of the group must have lagged behind, eventually leading to severing of ties; with time, distance grew, and the Hinduised Kharwars ceased to look upon the Santals as their kin.

As the caste system had initially developed on the basis of economic operations, so the economic operations have been diverting the tribes from the Hindu society divested of economic powers. For the same reason, the dominant Scheduled Tribes and Scheduled Castes would ever try to stall any attempt of the Government of withdrawing the concessions already granted to them. Already groups of privileged people are in existence in some of the major tribes and the perpetuation of concessions would be in their interest.

---

7. Dalton, E.T.: Descriptive Ethnology of Bengal, pp. 207-208.
8. Sinha, SC: State Formation and Rajput Myth in Tribal Central India, Man in India, Vol. 42.

With the development of an agricultural economy in the Gangetic and the eastern part of India since the 6th Century A.D., the advancing agricultural Hindu society denuded forests, making the aboriginal tribes retreat farther inside the jungles. At last, due to economic reasons, the tribals forsook their nomadic pattern of life and appeared in groups of agricultural labourers and with allied avocations. The impact of mixing with other societies-more advanced the ruthless-created an adverse impression on the tribal societies. Some of them gave in and gradually lifted themselves in the peripheral region of the dominant Hindu society, losing much of their tribal entities. The Pancham Varna was formed with such elements. Some others showed remarkable keenness in maintaining the tribal identity; the social resilience evinced during long periods of struggle for existence against disintegration has been stupendous. Tribals who failed to sustain landed property or failed to climb up the agricultural ladder formed the large bulk of labourers-agricultural or industrial, whereas the societies that could succeed in establishing themselves as permanent agriculture village community had stable societies and were eventually accepted in the larger Hindu fold even as Kshatriyas. This upgradation had actually taken place at a time when the dominant Hindu society was under severe stress. Inclusion of the converted Hindus enlarged the Hindu base.

In the third decade of the twentieth century, the anxiety of the Hindu society had reached a new height. With the apperance of Mahatma Gandhi in the Indian political scence, there emerged a conscious attempt at involving the down-trodden masses in the national movement. When Gandhiji joined the Home Rule League, leaders like M.R. Jayakar and M.A. Jinnah were not at all pleased. They were ill at ease and apprehensive of the consequences of such movements sponsored by Gandhiji. When the Home Rule League was converted to Swarajya Shabha, the distrust had accentuated. On October 27, 1920 Jinnah, Jayakar, K.M. Munshi and sixteen others left the Swarajya Sabha. Finally Jinnah left Congress at Nagpur Congress Conference in 1920. Gandhiji's way of involving the masses in movement was not liked by Jinnah; nor did the great Khilafat movement and non-cooperation movement please him. Muslim League came into being. Programmes chalked out by Jinnah appealed more to the religious susceptibilities of the Muslim community which eventually made a powerful thrust in obtaining political power as a group. This had added tension in the Hindu society.

The Santal tribe previously known as Kharwars had remained aloof for quite some time when an agricultural economy was developing around. They had retreated in the deep forests and were compelled to come out due to economic reasons and for sustenance. The Santal traditions speak of the tribe's wandering from place to place since its origin at Hihiri Pipiri, in quest of a permanent abode. The transformation from the pastoral to the village community system was first observed at Chae-Champa where they had re-organised their social organisation, as would be evident from the development of shibboleths. The newly- adopted village life was under rigid social control; nor was there any pressure on land. As such scattered homesteads are not to be found in the Santal villages. The clans indentified themselves with particular places and the settlements were on the basis of clans. The tribe settled itself as a semi-permanent agricultural community at Champa.

Unfortunately, the nucleated villages did not develop to the fullest extent. The pressure exerted on land by the Hindus made the tribals leave Champa for new places to settle, and the tribe once again reverted to the level of migratory agricultural society. After several generations they landed up at Saont where gradually they developed into a semi- permanent agricultural society once again. Even there, the pressure exerted by the Hindus led to a migration of the tribe. The oscillation between the migratory and the semi- permanent agricultural community status generated tensions in the community and the anxiety to retain tribal indentity in the face of so many odds came to the fore. Inspite of desperate endeavours like rising in arms against the landlords and the Government, the tribe has not yet been able to develop itself into a successful permanent agricultural society. The problem of land-alienation has been eating into its vitals and gradually the tribe is being huddled in areas having a concentration of the tribals. Much of the present-day tension owes its origin to this strife of the tribe aganist aliens. Once the tribe settled down as a permanent agricultural society, this tension would recede and the nation as a whole would gain tremendously.

Defeated and driven from place to place, without any domain of its own, the tribe has been showing definite trends to settle down for good, forsaking its nomadic entity. In fact, this nomadic trait itself was an imposition on the tribe. The tribe had earned a reputation as skilled agricultural labourer by the time the permanent settlement was brought in.

They had cleared extensive jungle-land into arable fields most of which they lost to the wily money lenders and mahajans later. For subsistence, they had to move from one place to the other, and as such, the nomadic pattern of life was not a matter of choice with them.

At the time of emergence of the tribe as a migratory agricultural village community, and even after that, during the settlement of the tribe in the Santal Parganas, land tenures were held by the Manjhies or the headmen who distributed the land to the members of the community. The holding was notionally held by the village community and every year, the land was supposed to be surrendered by all to the Manjhi who would again distribute the land for cultivation. Similarly, the Manjhi and other traditional village community officials were also supposed to resign their posts after which a nominal election would have been held to re-elect the Manjhi and other village officials. With the power to hold land for the community and with the subsequent allocation of some duties by the Magistrate of the district, the Manjhies came closer to the administration and gradually, the election of the Manjhi was reduced to a matter of course only. Caution impels me to mention here that there has all along been a rift between the family and the community in the Santal tribe, arising out of the failures of the traditional leadership. Religious individualism had pervaded the society threatening its cohesion. All the families developed their respective household Bongas or deities-Abge Bongas and Ora Bongas. Apart from these Bongas, the Santals started looking up at the Haprams or deceased ancestors for protection and help; they installed Hapram Bongas at their houses. The society was threatened with disintegration. The disreputed traditional leadership sought to resolve the problem by creating a new set of elites to interpret old traditional values to be invoked. The new elite was vested with a quasi-religious status and its mandates were to be carried through the social leadership in the person of the Manjhi and the More Hor. "Jaher Than" or the Sacred Grove was set up beyond the village boundary with a set of Bongas to be worshiped by the community as a whole. The worship of the Manjhi Haram (symbol of the traditional leadership) at the "Manjhi Than" within the village must precede the worship of the Bongas at the Jaher Than. Thus, the innovation stopped outside the village; within the village the Manjhi Haram reigns supreme. Individual families were allowed to continue their worship of the family deities and ancestors. Thereby a form of social control was enforced on all in the society in a bid to stop disintegration. Religion in the tribe did not develop into an organisation, able enough to attain controlling power. But it was used by the societal leadership as a tool to effect solidarity. Even during the aggressive overtures, the society and its leaders used religion as a tool of conditioning. The problem of social conditioning is that 'it is accepted as the reality by those who employ it, but then, as underlying circumstances change, the conditioning does not.'[9] All the charismatic leaders in the tribe had to overcome this constraint by providing alternatives lushed with projected compensatory rewards. The emerging new elites are also confronted with the same problem; the recognition of reality does not readily come from the society and members tend to continue in their earlier stance. The tribe, as also the individuals, disowned any responsibility in the waning economic condition or maladies.

---

9. Galbraith, J.K. : The Anatomy of Power (1984), p. 131.

As the tribe was not strong enough to spell out the perceived reasons of the woe, lest that would alienate the dominant Hindu neighbours, mundane failures were being probed in the supernatural. In the mundane plane the witch was created as a counterpoise to the Janguru or Sokha (the new elites as mentioned above). The Jangurus divined out the witches (Da-an), and after a village-trial the denounced witches were punished. The entire community became a defensive one. In this way, the tottering traditional leadership steadied itself with a new prop, inflicting pressure on families by finding out the witches-mostly women-and punishing them as the source of all evils. The public institutions of worship were thus created by the tribe in course of social reorganisation at Champa. It may be seen that the Santal society leaned more on the condign punishment than on compensatory rewards at the time of reorganising the society. Yet the conditioning was adequate as would be evident from the submission of the members to the social will, enhancing an internal solidarity. As power creates its own resistance, so new elites continued to come up. Personalities were projected, who in turn sought to create organisation to achieve its goal by bringing out the society from its shell. These personalities projected promises of compensatory rewards to all in the tribe, should they be successful in their venture of acquiring political power. The aggressive movements of the tribe were led by such personalities all through the ages.

By persistent efforts, some tribals could accrue rights over plots of land, and the Santals are obviously keen to adjust themselves to this new pattern of farm life. This changed pattern of life again has generated a stress in the society and a very high form of anxiety has been prevailing among them in view of the perceived threat from the environment. In fact, the alienation of land has been very extensive. As in the Barind in Malda District, an estimated area of 38.4 square miles was expropriated from the tribals (census 1951). The fact of land alienation from tribals had been admitted all along. To stem the tide of land-alienation, chapter vii (A) Bengal Tenanacy Act had been extended to the Santals of Malda even in 1923.

Under its provision no aborigine could transfer land by sale or mortgage without the Collector's permission. This impediment has since been overcome by a system of Khai-Khalasi (unufructuary mortgage) on unregistered deeds whereby money-lenders and non-agriculturists take physical possession of the cultivable land. The restitution of alienated land to the Santals that followed the movement of Jitu in Malda was limited to those plots that changed hands after 1923. To-day, many Santals would own more than fifteen acres of land on paper whereas the actual control may not go beyond two acres. Yet the official records may not reveal the sad plight, because the transfers are not noted in the official registers. Some tribals are working on the alienated land as share-croppers or almost on wages; this is also affecting the production- because the tribal would naturally pay more attention to the plot of land held by himself.

Land has been influencing the lives of the tribals so much that more than fifty per cent of cases of witch-accusations have land as a contributing factor. The lure of stability and prospect of getting land by division impel some tribals to level witch-accusations against relations. There are cases where sons did away with fathers just because the latter would not bequeath land to sons for sustenance after marriage. The significance of kinship is also dwindling sharply owing to extreme poverty. Owning land is a matter of status, the way to stability and freedom from fear.

There are no more urgent needs than those for food, drink, shelter, and protection from common dangers. The failure of men to satisfy these basic drives leads them over and over again not only to attempt to satisfy them in overt action but to formulate dreams of a more satisfactory condition in which there is either a rerturn to an imagined pristine purity or a construction of a new and perfect and everlasting society and culture. Hope is a catalyst. It spurs up dreams-dreams of stability, of fulfilment and progress. The ultimate goal of the society to take a sure place in the larger society with positive interactions beyond the community would seem a possibility.

The accrual of power and prestige would follow acquisition of a firm base on agricultural operations. The coming of the Santals in Barind was with great expectations that they would settle down there permanently.

For centuries, the tribe has been in quest of economic stability; the depredations of power of a dominant society in the surrounding had ever been its undoing. During a period of comparative calm and stability-perhaps at Champa- their imagination conjured up a social stratification along Hindu lines outlining imputed role definitions. The septs[1] were assigned particular work as in the Chaturvarnya among the Hindus. Kisku sept was allotted the task of the King; Soren became the Sipahi; Mandi a wealthy man corresponding to Baisya or Sresthi. While Hembram was of princely status, Murmu was given a priestly role. Hansda became the warrior, Tudu the Bandmaster, etc. However from the stratification it cannot be said for certain that the institution of kingship had actually developed among the Santals at that time. The social hierarchy nearly corresponded to that of ancient Vedic period when Kulapati, Vispati and Janapadapati held sway at various strata of the society—the Kula, the Vis and the Jana. The Santals had the head of family, the Manjhi (village headman) and the Parganait (head of a federation of villages). In the accounts of Kolean, the territory on both the banks of the Ganges was under the occupation of the Santals. Though the Hindus had defeated the Santals at Champa, the latter could recover their territory. Even during the Insurrection of 1855-56, the Santals could have driven away the Hindus but for the protection accorded to them by the British. The account of Kolean Guru clearly indicates that there had been an inaccurate appreciation about their real adversary and the sense of resilience against the Deko had clouded the thought of the Santal. His Golden Days were during his stay at Champa, which was perhaps characterised by the internal domination of the Parganas and Dihries, which was continued till the Santals carried on their depredations on adjoining lands in the plains after the harvest as mentioned in the annals of Hunter. In olden days the only payment to the chiefs was a basketful of grain, more an as offering rather than tax, like the 'bali' (an offering) prevalent among the Aryans. The Santal social leadership could not proceed further to assume the position of the King. As in the Vedic period, there would be elections to elect the headman, and like the Vedic system, the custom fell in disuse with the accumulation of powers into the hands of the leader. This phenomenon of not developing the stature of the leader to that of a King can be attributed to the factors that the tribe had to flee and live in isolation for a very long time and that it had to shift from place to place being under severe pressure from the advancing Hindus. We have already observed that the traditional leadership had been discredited for failures over and again. There is reason to believe that the system of Kingship had not developed among the Santals in the remote past. The Kisku was Rapaj, not the Raja (King). With the placement of performative 'pa', the connotation of the word changes to indicate that the Kisku was allotted to perform the duties of the Raja (King), not to be the King. Similarly, by inserting performative 'pi' to word Kisanr, performance of the duty of the treasurer is indicated by the word Kipisanr. Nor did such allotment of duties led to actual stratification of the septs on merits of power or prestige among themselves. The drag on the traditional leadership was, however, from within the society itself. It may be seen that the Manjhies were subjected to control by the More Hor all along which had its limitations in ideals and pursuits. A deep-seated antagonism does exist between the family and the societal leadership. But the pangs of fear and hunger touch all. Aspirations and search for security impel the development of new elites all along, keeping alive the struggle for leadership. Orans suggested the role of envy as a disintegrative force. Conceding that, it might perhaps be pointed out that envy has distrust at its base, affecting solidarity.

The legends of the tribe are replete with stories of kings, queens and princes. This phenomenon may be explained away as the projection of the dream of the tribe, of the urge to acquire power whereby the maladies could be removed.

It is to be noted that tribal aristocrats happened to embrace Hinduism before the laeity-a fact discernible in other aboriginal tribes as well. The legend that the tribe had left Shikharbhum as the King set up himself as a Rajput, may also be recalled. The idea of kingship is an extension of Hindu influence on the Santals. To the tribal, it is synonymous to power-that-be which can remove the maladies of the tribe.

We have observed that during the re-organisation of society, the Santals opted for the group leadership and imposed such leadership on the society by creating a new set of elites dependent on the traditional social leadership. The new set of elites acted as a prop to the tottering social leadership. The source of power in the society was the solidarity effected through conditioning and corresponding submission. In winning submission, the tribe had to lean more on the condign power than on its compensatory aspect. The power was decentralised in the villages where the temporal leadership was under the control of the More Hor. Setting up of separate Jaher Than for each village heightened the identity of the village. The separative tendency went to the extent of debarring a villager from offering or performing worship at the Jaher Than of the next village even. The village leadership zealously guarded the power vested in them. The leadership of the Parganait has never been total. Only in the Dihri, on special occasions like Disam Sendra, the authority of the Manjhi and village leadership relented and that too, for a short duration. Thus, the Santals combine as a community on special occasions only and for leading the community during upheavals or emergency, the charismatic leaders emerge who hold sway over the village leadership and other forms of community leadership. In normal times, the village leadership takes over. The defensive shell of the society stands on the way of new ideas permeating within the Community and the compulsions of long conditioning exert themselves. Thus the traditional village leadership could not develop beyond village level. That is one of the reasons why the village leadership could not keep pace with the changing time.

The Santals conceived personality as a source of power. Religion did not develop into an organisation that could attune the tribe towards obtaining political power. So the tribe projected personalities. The institution of Hapram Bonga is essentially a form of personality cult, not to speak of Abge Bongas and Orak Bongas. The resultant religious individualism was sought to be curbed by the social reorganisation at Champa, thereby stifling the personality cult to a secondary social position-individuals were allowed to worship these Bongas but had to accept the community Bongas as also the Manjhi Haram (symbol o. traditional leadership) as social responsibility. On the mundane plane, under normal conditions the Manjhi is the personality in whom power is vested. But the Manjhi is working with serious limitations-he is controlled by the More Hor. Envy and distrust shackle him to the village society, and power is shared by the More Hor. Jealousy which is anti-thetic to possessions of all mundane attributes, cuts at the root of accummulation of wealth and consequential power in the village community.

Prior to embarking on an aggressive overture or movement, the personality arranges conditioning of the ideas through organisation and holds prospect of compensation in case it won political power. Such personalities are evidently synthetic ones, combining the temporal and the spiritual aspects of leadership; the traits of the personality are embellished and sustained by myths and legends giving out glimpses of the social intention. The process of explicit conditioning proceeds to the implicit, and expectations and hope lead to an ephemeral but willing suspension of disbelief and distrust, with corresponding increase in submission to the projected will of the personality thus created. But the sustenance of personality clashes with the idea of the decentralisation of power; exercise of power by the personality generates resistance, and the internal submission to the personality cracks with external vicissitudes. The social attitude of the Santals stood on the way of relenting to personality. Yet, in emergency, or in long spells of deprivation and discomfiture, the tribe submitted to personalities who led them during the stormy days, be it the insurrection of 1855-56 or the days of Jitu in 1924 onwards. During such movements, the society allowed the leader an exercise of unlimited power on society, breaking social norms even, as it happened in 1855-56. This surrender to the extension of power of the individual, even though irrational, helped in the development of the charismatic leaders who tended to assume total leadership of the movement. With the removal of the leaders from the scene, the tribe reverted to its social mooring. As land was the main issue-that being the prime necessity of establishing a permanent agricultural village society-so power is associated with the personality that dispenses and controls land as a source of income. In bid to achieve such power for the well-being of the tribe, the members relented to the personality that led the struggle. Assumption and control of power by personality gave rise to the institution of the King. The institution has to be sustained against external onslaughts, which the Santals failed to do on both the occasions known to us. The idea of Santal Raj came to the surface at least twice-once during the Hul of 1855-56 under Sido-Kanhu, and during 1927-32 in Barind under the leadership of Jitu Sardar. The movements of Diba and Kisun of Seraikela-Mayurbhanj had assumed the character of peasant rebellion and it is not known for certain if they had similarly wanted to set up their own Raj there as well. The divergence of social attitudes-to maintain the strength of the group against the individual and surrendering to the arbitrary authority of the charismatic leader, may seem paradoxical. Under normal conditions the society wielded absolute power as a community. The power extended to extreme exercise of condign power in dispensing with a-social human elements by ostracising or liquidation even. This power is not allowed to any individual; such extreme decisions are invariably collective. The society always held the personality in check at all levels of social leadership through councils. Under extraordinary conditions, however, this power is wielded by the charismatic leader whose mandates run through the entire society. Along with conditioning through organisation, condign power is resorted to for bringing about total submission, and to weed out recalcitrant elements as well. This happens only during large scale movements in which the society at large participates to express the aggressive position of the society against external adversaries.

While many other tribes gradually lost their tribal identity by merging with the Hindu society, the Santals retained their tribal identity with ferocious zeal. To fight against disintegration, the tribe availed of the defensive stance as a strategy. This defensive stance was necessary to counter the disintegrative forces which arose out of an oscillation of the tribe between the stages of migratory agricultural community and the semi-permanent agricultural community. The object of the tribe was to establish itself as a permanent agricultural society. The rigid social control gave rise to resistance; The deepening misery added to the troubles of the tribe. In response to the intense social will to escape from the maladies, charismatic leaders emerged, leading the way to a definite purpose. The social control gave way to the arbitrary control of the charismatic leader, withdrawing the rigours of control on the society. Out of the defensive shell of society, there was an onrush towards the external enemy.

The entire society became aggressive. Yet there was a return to the defensive stance. With the defeat in the aggressive endeavour, the society reverted to its defensive shell, adjusting to new circumstances for external necessities, retaining its internal solidarity to the most. The traditional leadership took over. There was, however, a new group of men who poundered over the causes of failure in the Hul of 1855-56. The mundane failure was being probed in the supernatural, and out of this train of thought, emerged Bhagirath Manjhi of Godda Subdivision in the Santal Parganas. The Santal mind again bridged the supernatural to the mundane plane, attributing the failure to human frailties and aberrations. The Sapha Hor movement was launched, largely inducting Hindu ideas of pollution and purification. Out of this movement, the eventual rise of the Satyam Shibam Sect in Barind in Malda district can be traced. It may be seen later that Jitu's movement had all the signs of the tribal method of resurgence-defensive society turned aggressive and after defeat, reverted to its defensive shell, the rigour's of social control tightening all over. In the experience of the Santals, the personality could not overcome the societal resistance in the accumulation and concentration of wealth, power and prestige under normal conditions, to be the source of all power enveloping the tribe over any geographical area. The Santal society was the main obstacle to the personality in attaining the stature of the King.

The aboriginal tribal societies continued to be attracted to the Hindu society, the exploitation and inequalities nevertheless. "The economic and social arrangements that had been built up in India from ancient times on the basis of village agriculture and handicrafts and the protection of the rights of each in his ancestral calling, were of a kind that they enabled people to survive in spite of the many vicissitudes through which they passed over the centuries. Inspite of the prevalence of inequalities between the different 'Jatis' and between the 'Varnas', because they enjoyed the basic material securities and because they could observe without let or hindrance their family, caste and local customs, the common people did not protest against the social supremacy enjoyed by the brahmins. Because the brahminically governed Aryan society recognised the rights of people to their own customs, the incoming communities freely accepted the positions assigned to them in Hindu society.

There is no doubt that the brahminically governed society was economically better off than the society of the Kols and the Juangs. Mainly because of this attraction and because of the assurance that they would not need to alter their own customs radically, we see the Juangs, Oraons and other communities gradually abandoning their independence and moving towards brahminical society."[10]

The inexorable drawing in of the aborigines towards Hinduism has been very slow, but sure. The vast masses of the Shudras had been drawn from the aborigines to a great extent, to facilitate the extending agricultural economy and allied

10. Bose, N.K. : The Structure of Hindu Society, p. 114.

avocations. Only when in danger from extraneous sources, the Hindus allowed induction of aborigine ethnic groups with a premium-allowing such groups higher status of Kshatriyas. The groups thus inducted had maintained their group solidarity at the time of induction, and had earned renown for their military prowess. Later when the Hindu society had lost absolute control over the economic activities, they inducted those communities as Kshatriyas who had maintained their group solidarity and could establish themselves as permanent agricultural societies. Thus, it would be evident that the Hindu society reacted to changes in situation and adjusted itself to fight for its own existence.

A close look at the Santals as a tribe would reveal the tremendous potentiality of the community. The valiant tribe could preserve its group solidarity to a remarkable degree in spite of the vicissitudes over centuries. From a murky past, the tribe obtained the first foot-hold as an agricultural community at Chae-Champa and reorganised its society. It is at Champa that the tribe created 'Khunts' or sub-septs. They fought their way up, retaining a firm will to maintain their tribal identity. The capability of reorganising the society along defensive line by introducing new elements like Sokha and its counterpoise the witch, in order to bolster the traditional leadership by suitable props is an ingenuity. This mechanism was used by the tribe to stop disintegration during periods that followed the aggressive and warlike moves to establish themselves as a permanent agricultural society. The mechanism helped the tribe to re-group itself after major upheavals. Without a definite social will to surge ahead as a group, this would not have been possible. Another significant indication may perhaps be noted here that while the traditional leadership controlled the society in its defensive stance, the aggrerssive external moves were led by new elites arising out of the society. These elites had been formed as Subah during the insurrectioin led by Sido-Kanhu, and were charismatic leaders of the tribe during emerging upheavals. The growth-rate in population is also a helpful factor. That the tribe had taken to the defensive stances deliberately would be evident from the myths created by them that they had left places to save the honour of the womenfolk, or religion. In effect, they were forced out of their possessions by members of the dominant society and they were trying to settle themselves without much success. To retain their possession or privileges, they had taken to violence at times, followed by a return to the defensive shell. In the initial stages of their aggresive roles, the tribe had failed to identify the real adversary, as would be evident from the murder of Cleveland. The gain out of this incident was almost nothing except being an expression of the restive social mind of the tribals. Shri Dhirendranath Baskey attributed a spirit of independence that resulted into the organisation of Tilka Manjhi's group and murder of Cleveland (January 13, 1784). He has also mentioned that the Santals were averse to paying taxes to the East India Company, contrary to their practice of living free in the jungle. The demand of taxes was an imposition which was not done even in the Mughal days. Tilak Murmu had organised a resistance against the oppressors who had been doing immense harm to the Santals by exacting taxes.[11] The demand of tax might have enraged the Santals. But the action of Tilak Murmu was by no means indicative of any intention to oust the foreign rulers, nor was it followed by any attempt at setting up a Santal Raj. It may be recalled that it was only in 1832 that the Damin-i-Koh was thrown open to the Santals, and the number of Santals living around before that year was rather meagre.

The titanic struggle of 1855-56 revealed much of the social will in a more pronounced manner. The idea of the Santal Raj found its expression for the first time. The enemy was identified, the object was clearer. The expression indicated the desirability of wielding the power that is associated with the Raj or the King, by the Santals for the welfare of the common man, for, the Raj or the King had failed them to give protection. Appreciation of this role of the King or state is a new phenomenon in the history of the tribe. It is generally held that the Santals had no definite political ideal before them when they rose in revolt. It has also been held that the insurrection was primarily against the oppressions of the money-lenders

11. Baskey, D.N.: Santal Ganasangramer Itihas, pp.12-15.

and Deko that resulted into land-alienation and extreme misery. But it is during this process of revolt that the leaders acknowledged the role of a source of power in the King (Raja) or Government, unlike the skirmish led by Tilka Majhi. During this insurrection, the proclamations issued by the Santal leadership to various officials would be a sure indication of their will of establishing a Santal Raj. The following proclamation issued to the Commissioner, Magistrate and like Government officials would indicate that at one point of the insurrection, the Santals had transcended the role of rebels and projected to have established a kingdom or Raj for themselves. The proclamation runs thus:

> "shibŝhaha bhagatsubā sambhābita rājār ajna"
> ramjio lāl desh jay kariāchhen tannimitta āmi likhitechhi, tumi āmāke jānāibe je judge magistrate O collectorerā juddha karane manastha kāriachhen Kina ? jadi āmārdiger subārā ākraman kare tabe raiyatdiger kshati haibek ebong jadi ingrej senārā aise tathācha rāiyātrā klesh pāibe, ataeba ihā juktisiddha je kebal kishoriā subār sahit ingrājerā juddha karun, tāhā haile raiyatdiger kona hani haibek nā, ei parwanār karma dākjoge oi sakal lokdigake jnāta kara jāhārdiger nimitta ihā lekhā haila.
>
> serestādārke lekhā jai."[12]

The proclamation was written in kayethi Hindi, and the above translation in Bengali appeared in the Samvad Bhaskar on February 5, 1856.

The above proclamation called upon the officials to convey if they wanted war. In the event of attack launched by the rebels the raiyats would suffer. Same would be the result if the British army took the offensive. It was suggested that the British army might engage itself with the army of Kishoria Subah in which event no harm would reach the raiyats.

---

12. Saontal Bidroha Theke Operation Barga (Board of Revenue, Govt. of West Bengal), p. 28.

The assumption of the kingship, and the expression of the directives of the King-to-be-anointed, reveal genuine concern for the raiyats. It also reveals the belief in the strength of the rebel army which was in a position to launch attack. The point of submission is that the Santals had by that time comprehended the role definitions of the King of kingship and its moral responsibility towards the raiyats in protecting them from destruction. The "Reak Katha" which was completed in 1871, also supports this contention when it ascribed the intention to the rebels of doing away with the Kings and the money-lenders and driving away of the Hindus to the other side of the Ganges, to establish their kingdom. As the people started the insurrection, many charismatic leaders came to the fore.[13] It is evident that a social will to establish a kingdom for themselves had clearly emerged out by the time of the Santal Insurrection 1855-56. Yet, during the insurrection the Santals devised their plans along tribal reckoning.

Orans suggested a deeper intent behind the rebellion of 1855-56 than the relief from the said economic plight. He quotes McPherson in support of his assumption. "Although the officially ascertained causes of the rebellion were the grievances above related, it is now generally recognised that a deeper, or at any rate, a supervening cause was the Santhal yearning for independence, a dream of the ancient days when they had no overlords, perhaps a memory of the pre-historic times when according to some speculators they were themselves masters of the Gangetic valley and had not yet been driven back by the Aryan invaders. Be that as it may, there has been observed at various times a peculiar movement amongst the Santhals to which the name 'Kherwarism' has been given. 'Kherwar' according to the Rev. Mr. Skrefsrud' is the ancient tribal name of the Santhals and in their minds is inseparably associated with the golden era of their history, namely, the time when they lived in Champa in absolute independence and had no rent or tribute to pay, but only to bring a small annual offering to their leaders in virtue of their office.' Ordinarily Santhals are quiet and contented, but when any grievance rankles in

13. M.H.R.K., p. 92.

their minds, the spirit of unrest arises and their leaders or self-interested agitators appeal to the ancient traditions of the race and the hope of independence. On this subject Mr. Oldham writes, 'It (the yearning for independence) is not the popularly received cause of the insurrection of 1855; but after reading all the correspondence connected with the introduction of the Santals into the Damin-i-Koh, and its administration by Mr. Pontet, till the rising, the large part which this idea and hope played in that outbreak becomes plain to my mind. The movement so originated drew to it all those whose patriotism was stimulated by the recollection of their suffering at the hands of the usurers and the police; but the fundamental idea at work and that which was attempted to be put in practice was the establishment of a Santal realm and kingdom."[14]

The above was written by McPherson in his final Report on the Survey and Settlement Operations in the District of Santal Parganas, 1898-1907 (Calcutta 1909; pages 37-8), much later than the actual Sapha Hor movement was initiated by Bhagrit Baba in 1871. Later in the case of Jitu, we shall find that during the decades of agitation and struggle against the oppressors and finally against the British Raj, Jitu and his compatriots had taken advantage of the train of agitations and movements against the British Raj in the country, adjusting themselves to prevailing circumstances in stages, to declare independence. The aggressive roles thus played by the tribe display gradual development of a political awareness associated with a revival of the tribe, with its tribal identity and core in tact. Failures had impelled the tribe to switch back to the defensive shell. But throughout, the tribe has been able to maintain its tribal solidarity. Progress enabled coming up of the new elites, and a state of perennial excitement and tension has been allowed to continue. It is due to the distance from the dominant society that this tension is not readily reckoned. But incidents of witch-killings, village trials etc. are definite signs of tension in the social body. This tension is also forcing the community to adopt programmes. Nature of demands or

---

14. Culshaw, W.J. & Archer, W.G.:The Santal Rebellion, Man in India, Vol. XXL, No.4, pp. 228-229.

objects has a direct bearing to the stratification of the society. The established elites or traditional leadership would want status quo, the new elite assured of his position would seek prestige, while the laeity would ever clamour for a steady means of subsistence i.e. income. New ideas are not readily accepted by the laeity, because he finds security in the system in which he has been attuned to. Besides, the traditional leadership acts as a screen. This has been the experience of all ethnic groups trying for improvement to come to terms with the dominant social group.

The rebellion of 1855-56 had extended over Bhagalpur, Birbhum and the area as reckoned Santal Parganas presently. Similar tension and excitement had ruled other parts of the adjoining province as well giving rise to rebellions.

Orans mentions the southern Santal tradition of Seraikela regarding a rebellion in the latter part of the nineteenth century. The traditions speak of the exploits of two brothers, Diba and Kisun. The Santals of Mayurbhanj also share the tradition. It is said that about 60 Parganas had taken part in the rebellion, but the actual extent of the area could not be ascertained specifically. The rebellion attracted the attention of the administration to the necessity of ameliorative actions. Orans writes, "At the same time, the Santals must have recognized after these defeats that under prevailing conditions, increased political power and improvement in rank were not to be obtained by military mights. Evidence to be presented later suggested that this recognition contributed to a decline in solidarity".[15]

The above observation of Orans is not borne by the experience in the case that is going to be discussed in the following chapters. In the movement of Jitu, the emulative factors had been used to strengthen solidarity of the tribe progressing in a particular direction. It may, however, be suggested that failures in a particular programme led the tribe to change its tactical and strategic approach to the goal in view. Alternative channels were found out by the persistent tribe to achieve its objective.

15. Orans, Martin: The Santal: A Tribe in Search of A Great Tradition.

Chapter 3

District : Malda

District Malda is situated between latitudes 25° 32′ 08" and 24° 40′ 20" in the northern hemisphere, and to the north of the Tropic of Cancer. In ancient times the district was in the country Pundravardhana which formed a part of the Mauryan empire. In Gupta Age, it was a Bhukti or administrative division of the empire. Sasanka, a contemporary of Harshavardhana, was known as the Lord of Gaur. It is difficult to trace the history of the district till the advent of Gopala who was a man of Barendri, a tract of country situated between the Ganges and the Karatowa. Both the Palas and the Senas were known as Gaureswaras. Subsequently, Gaur passed into the hands of the Muslims, and the British Raj.

The district of Malda came into being under the British informally only in 1813, although the East India Company had obtained the Diwani of the Subah of Bengal-Bihar-Orissa from Emperor Shah Alam in 1765. The creation of the district was effected by taking parts of Purnea, Dinajpur and Rajshahi, as certain thanas were crime-affected. A Joint-Magistrate was posted at Malda and the thanas of Shibgunj, Kaliachak, Bholahat, Gurguribah of the Purnea District, the thanas of Malda, Bamangola of the district of Dinajpur and the thanas of Rohanpur and Chuppye of the district of Rajshahi were left in his charge. The newly formed district was included in Bhagalpur Division. A Treasury was established at Malda in 1832, from which year the separate existence of the district is usually reckoned. But it was only in 1859 that a Magistrate and Collector was placed in charge of the district. In 1875 the district boundaries were notified. 65 villages from Murshidabad and 237 villages from Dinajpur were transferred to Malda district.

The district comprised of fifteen police stations. The areas given in the table below include the diara strip of 401 square miles surveyed in 1916-18 during the Rajshahi Settlement Operations. It should be noted that owing to the omission of decimals from the figures below, the total area of the district has been shown as 1987 sq. miles, whereas the actual area to the nearest square mile was 1986. The following were the police stations:-

Harishcandrapur	150	Manikchak	113
Kharba	142	Kaliachak	209
Gazole	198	Sibgunj	183
Bamangola	68	Bholahat	48
Habibpur	153	Gomastapur	123
Old Malda	87	Nachole	110
English Bazar	98	Nawabganj	149
Ratua	156		

In 1879 the district was transferred from the Judgeship of Dinajpur to that of Rajshahi. Up to 1876 the district formed part of Rajshahi Division, and between 1876 and 1905 the district formed part of Bhagalpur Division which was then in Bengal. In 1905 the district was transferred from Bhagalpur Division to Rajshahi Division on the formation of the Provinces of Eastern Bengal and Bihar. In 1912, when the partition of Bengal was annulled, it was included in the Rajshahi Division till August 1947. On the 15th August 1947, the fate of the district was uncertain. On the 17th August it was found that the district would be partitioned, the thanas of Shibgunj, Nawabganj, Bholahat, Nachole and Gomastapur being transferred to Pakistan. The above- mentioned thanas are presently in Bangladesh. The present area of Malda district, according to the Surveyor General, is 1436 square miles.

River Mahananda happens to be the traditional boundary between Rarh and Barendra. The area to the east of the Mahananda is known as Barind even today. The country to the West of the Mahananda has again been divided in two parts-Tal and Diara. South of Kalindri is the most fertile land of the district, the Diara, and most populous too. The Tal is a low-lying area where flood is incidental to rise in water- level in the Kalindri or other tributaries of the Ganges; swamps and marshes are in plenty. The Barind is characterised by high land with old alluvium soil, with water- courses running down the valleys. It is also divided in two parts-the danga (high land) and the doba (low lying land).

The forest in Barind had disappeared barring a few stretches here and there, and the Katal, after five decades of clearing by the Santals. Pemberton in the course of his revenue survey in the middle of the nineteenth century came across extensive stretches of jungles and marshes which were full of various wild animals including rhinoceros and different species of birds. He also mentioned tiger, leopard, tiger cat, the monkey, the porcupine, the hare, the sambhar, the barasinga deer, the spotted deer, the antelope, the hog deer, the wild buffaloe, the wolf, the pole cat, the civet cat, etc. Hunter observes," the ruins of Gaur and Pandua are the favourite haunts not only of tigers, but of every other beast, bird and reptile which frequent the isolated jungles of Bengal. The Katal (Barind) which is estimated to cover about 150 square miles in this district, particularly that portion between the Tangan and the Punarbhava rivers, is also entirely given up to wild animals. The jungle is too dense in many cases to admit even the passage of an elephant and consequently the larger beasts of prey breed almost undisturbed"[1].

The Santals came to Barind to clear the jungle and break the land for cultivation. After five decades of assiduous work, not much of forest was left in the district, particularly in the Barind except a few patches of Sal trees and Katal that could not be converted into arable fields.

There was a District Board in the district. Till 1930, the District Board was entirely nominated. The first elected Board was formed in 1931 with 12 elected and 6 nominated members.

---

1. As quoted in District Gazetteers- Malda, 1969 (Ed. J.C. Sengupta)

The following were the elected members:-

1. Shri Keshab Charan Kaur, Pleader, Englishbazar.
2. Shri Ramesh Chandra Das, Teacher, Chanchal H.E.School.
3. Shri Md. Fakirullah Mian, Motwali, Lakhipur Waqf Estate, Amnura, Nawabganj.
4. Shri Jahur Ahmed Chaudhuri, Zamindar, Monakosha, Shibganj.
5. Shri Kanti Charan Basu, Manager, Shershabad Estate of Maharaja of Mymensing at Kansat.
6. Shri Taheruddin Mohammad, Pleader, Nawabganj.
7. Shri Govinda Chandra Thakur, Jotedar, Amriti, English bazar.
8. Shri Latif Ahmed Mian, Jotedar, Amriti, Englishbazar.
9. Shri Abdul Wahed Biswas, Pleader, Englishbazar.
10. Shri Elias Mohammad, Pleader, Englishbazar.
11. Shri Pramatha Nath Misra, Pleader, Englishbazar.
12. Shri Idris Ahmed Mian, Jotedar, Durlavpur Shibganj.

The nominated members were :-

1. Sub-Divisional Officer (Ex-officio)-to represent Harischandrapur Thana.
2. District Inspector of Schools (Ex-officio).
3. Rai Bahadur Panchanan Majumdar-to represent Bholahat and Englishbazar.
4. Rev. Father Cattaneo to-represent Santals of Gazole Bamangola-Habibpur-Malda.
5. Md. Emaduddin, Pleader, Englishbazar.
6. Reazuddin Ahmed, Pleader, Englishbazar and Manikchak.

It may be observed that the Santals had no representation through a tribal nominee, though it was felt necessary to safeguard the interests of the tribals. The Santal problem was a burning one, and the tribal leaders that emerged had no acceptance to the district administration. It will be seen in subsequent chapters that Jitu had established himself as a charismatic leader by the time of this nomination to father Cattaneo. But he was not acceptable to the administration. The attitude of the district administration was amply revealed in the note in the District Gazetteers that "All this would never have taken place if the Santals were not so astonishingly credulous and if Jitu's activities could have been lilmited". In fact, the leaders among the tribals had come in confrontation with the administration when defying the order promulgated under section 144 Criminal Procedure Code in May 1927. More than 3000 Santals attended the worship of goddess Kali on that occasion. The administration had all along been trying to curb the activities of Jitu by prosecuting him under several criminal cases and prosecutions.

The non-acceptance of the emerging tribal leaders to the administration was spurred up by the tribals' taking up cue from the non-cooperators in the district, of course in their reckoning. The mutual cordial relationship between the tribals and the administration had shown cracks after the former had shown preference to the nationalist movement. Only coercive methods were thought of in bringing the Santals away from active politics.

There were eight High Schools in the district none in the Barind. Against 31 Government-aided Middle English Schools, there were two M.E. Schools managed by the District Board and five unaided M.E. Schools. There was one aided girls' M.E. School at Sadar (Barlow Girls' School) of which the Collector was the President. There was a large number of Primary Schools.

There was a Santal Board of Education of which the Collector was the President. The other members were the District Inspector of Schools and the Chairman of the District Board.

Considering the percentage of literacy among Santals, it may be said that the Board did not achieve much. But the constitution of the board with the highest district officials is indicative of the importance attached to welfare of the tribals.

The Board was set up in 1923 to look after the educational needs of the Santals. By 1934, the Board had established 31 Santal Primary Schools in areas where Santals were living. In his report, Shri K.C.Barman gave a list of these schools thus :-

Habibpur police station	15
Gazole police station	10
Gomostapúr police station	2
Bamongola	
Harischandrapura	One each
Nawabganj	
Nachole	

All these schools received contributions from the Government as well as from the District Board. Generally, the attendance was disappointing. Most of the teachers did not know Santali at all. The medium of instruction was Bengali. Christian missionaries had also started a few Primary Schools for Santal boys.[2]

The excise revenue in 1930-31 was about two lakh on the previous year. The reason was attributed to economic depression. The civil disobedience movement could not make much headway in the district due to harsh handling of the district administration. It is significant to note that excise revenue drops prior to wide spread trouble in areas whose tribals live in large homogenous groups. Intense poverty of the tribals precludes the possibility of purchase, and during such times home-brewing increases in the community. During the period, the revenue from Tari had a sharp drop from Rs. 33265/- to Rs. 18987/- revenue on account of Pachwai had a drop from Rs. 4024/- to Rs. 1365/- only. Santals normally do not take

2. Barman, K.C., Report on the Condition of the Santhals in Malda 1934, p. 7.

country-spirit and drop of revenue on that account may be attributed to less consumption by other communities. Similar drop in revenue was noticed during 1927-28 when there followed a dispute between the tribals and the administration over worship of Goddess Kali in Malda. During that period, Jitu and his associates had declared 'independence' in Barind as well. In the district, distress had intensified from 1929, with a sense of morality closely following the heels. In fact, the tribals were averse to payng license fee for the home- brewing and took the opportunity of stopping payment at troubled times. The revenue collected on accont of Pachwai since 1921 would be a pointer to that. From 1921 onwards, the yearly revenue of the district for Pachwai were Rs. 694, 1750, 1755, 4819, 1196, 2952, 373, 5657, 4024 and 1365 for financial year 1930-31. The fall in revenue corresponded with large-scale troubles or movements of the Santals.

In 1930, the district was divided into ten Revenue Thanas and fifteen Police Stations. The sanctioned strength of the district police was one Superintendent, four Inspectors, 33 Sub-Inspectors, 43 Assistant Sub-Inspectors and 332 Constables, making the total 413. It must be admitted that the strength was not adequate to police an area of 1986 square miles, divided into 15 thanas, with very limited transport facilities. All the cases had to be brought to the district headquarters as there was only one sub-Division in the district.

The case-work was not heavy. The following chart will reveal the position adequately :-

Year	1921	1922	1923	1924	1925	1926	1927	1928	1929	1930
All offences	615	504	639	761	750	1036	861	832	948	683
Offences against public tranquililty.	7	32	50	46	73	49	1	18	12	33
Bad livelihood	12	10	30	48	100	43	73	66	100	35
Keeping the peace	-	32	2	8	4	1	3	5	19	30

It would be seen that the outbreak of dacoities and burgalaries in Gazole Circle (i.e. Barind) in 1926 and 1927 finds a reflection in the figures pertaining to those years. It would also appear that rioting had significantly increased in the years 1923 and 1925. The prosecutions under the preventive sections of law also showed an upward trend and would reveal the endeavour of the administration in maintaining law and order. It may be mentioned that Jitu had also been prosecuted twice under the Bad Livelihood Clauses (110 Criminal Procedure Code).

The work-load in the criminal courts showed an upward trend, though the increase in the Sessions Courts was not that remarkable, taking from 1921 to 1930 (an increase by 75 per cent in ten years, the numbers being 12 and 21). The work-load of the Stipendiary Magistrates increased too (from 505 in 1921 to 1081 in 1930). The Honorary Magistrates had an average case-work of 300 cases a year, though in 1930 it suddenly had a drop to 143 cases against 197 persons. The work-load of the Stipendiary Magistrates had jumped up to 1081 cases against 2060 persons. It appears that during a period of major stress, the local police had small matters ignored.

The work in the Civil Courts had been heavier. The average disposal of civil suits was about 9000 cases a year. This figure includes disposal of petitions as well. During 1930, this figure increased by 1757 cases. Needless to say that the Santals went unrepresented mostly as they were not litigant in nature. Apart from that, it was almost a recognised practice among the litigant Hindus to obtain exparte decree from the Courts by arranging to suppress the notices. The high rate of disposal was possible on account of this factor"[3].

Apart from the Stipendiary Magistrates, the following honorary magistrates used to sit in three Benches :-

A. Sadar Independent Bench—

1. Rai Sahib Peari Lal Neogi	Single Sitting	1st class
2. Shri Pramatha Nath De	Single Sitting	2nd class

---

3. Figures obtained from Census.

3. Moulvi Jahur Ahmed Chaudhuri	Single Sitting	3rd class
4. Shri Ashutosh Chaudhuri	Single Sitting	3rd class
5. Rai Saheb Jadunandan Chaudhuri	Single Sitting	3rd class
B. Old Malda Bench—		
6. Shri Rajani Kanta Das	Single Sitting	3rd class
7. Shri Girija Kanta Das	Joint Sitting	3rd class
C. Nawabganj Independent Bench-		
8. Shri Sris Chandra Moulik,	Single Sitting	3rd class

Besides these Benches, there were Union Courts at—

1. Kotwali within Englishbazar Police Station
2. Chowki Mirdadpur Within Manikchak Police Station

3. Mathurapur	"	"
4. Araidanga	"	Ratua Police Station
5. Chanchal	"	Kharba Police Station
6. Malatipur	"	"
7. Kansat	"	Shibgunj Police Station.

It was felt by the administration that the Santals were being fleeced ruthlessly by the money-lenders, the landlords and their agents, taking advantages of the Santal's dread for the Court. The system was alien to him, and he could not make himself understood. Money was another constraint for him. The lawyers did not make a kindlier lot. It was felt that the matters pertaining to the Santals should not be referred to the Civil Court; rather their cases should come to the Collector who was keen to establilsh a direct contact with the tribals, like in Santal Parganas.Summary trial would have been better to dispense with ready justice which the tribal appreciated most. That system would have the additional advantage of spot enquiry through the Collector's officials. Reports were sent to the Government to that effect but the proposal did not materialise.

In 1894-97, Malda district was in Bhagalpur Division. There was no Santal Chowkidar or Daffadar in the district. They came from the Dosadh, Hari, Teor, Khamaroo, Rajbanshi and Muhammadan communities. It was not that there was any embargo on appointing Santals as Chowkidars. The Santal hamlets around that time were too small, and the Santal population was also negligible in comparison to other communities. Incidence of crime was not that high either. Around that time, in Santal Parganas, there were 274 Santal Chowkidars as against 1044 Doms, 668 Ghatwals and 285 Pahariyas. With the growth of population in Barind, the number of rural police gradually increased. In 1930, there were 1332 Chowkidars and 182 Daffadars in the district. The four thanas of Barind had 239 Chowkidars and 32 Daffadors. In the Santal-dominated areas, Chowkidars and Daffadors appointed were Santals, though men from Kamar, Turi and Kora communities were also appointed. During the days of non-cooperation movement, the rural police found it difficult to discharge their duties in the village. Owing to the weekly attendance at the police stations, however, a line of communication with the administration could be kept open.

The non-co-operation movement launched by Congress had its impact in Malda district as well. The programme of introducing 'charka' (spinning wheel) and desisting from paying rents and taxes caught on with the sullen populace. Difficulties were experienced with regard to Chowkidari tax in Malda, Midnapur, Rangpur and Faridpur. Complainants and witnesses in cases against Congress volunteers were being boycotted or intimidated in Malda. Collection of money for Khilafat Fund through meetings were in progress. In the second week of April 1922, rupees 460 was collected from Shibganj alone. The rural police was also intimidated by villagers asking them to resign. One Daffadar and one Chowkidar resigned from services in the last week of April 1922. The rural police was restive for inadequate and irregular pay. The chowkidars in Bamangola Thana were planning a strike in August 1922 to press their demand for pay-rise. Instances of chowkidars being socially boycotted for refusing to resign their posts were reported from the district as well as from Tippera in September 1922. Pressure from public accentuated their plight and the meagre pay was hardly any compensation for the troubles the chowkidars were having. At this time, the unrest in police affected them more.

Policemen had their grievances. The social apathy coupled with inadequate pay broke their reserve, and they also started putting forth their demands for higher wages. In fact, around that time, Congress was trying to impress upon the policemen to resign their posts. Anonymous letters and handbills were being distributed in police barracks, urging them to leave the barracks and not to help the tyrants against their own countrymen. Congress leaders were thinking of exerting their personal influences to impress policemen to that end. It was hoped that about 5000 policemen would resign from Bengal at the request and appeal was issued by Dr. Rajendra Prasad. Serious discontent was noticed among policemen in Malda in April 1922. Leaflets and post cards urging policemen to revolt against the Raj were distributed in various districts. Some leaflets were distributed by purported policemen urging colleagues to be in readiness to act-to resign-in case the Raj did not increase their pay from Rs. 20 to Rs. 50 per month. Some leaflets indicated that reportedly some constables had already given up their jobs in protest of the inhuman policy of torture by the Government. Leaflets were in Hindi and Bengali. Some anonymous petitions were kept at the door of a shop at Palong Police Station in Faridpur district, stating that the Constabulary would submit resignation and would hand in their kit on 1 July 1930, unless their pay was increased. Two postcards were received at Malda Police Lines. A major trouble had taken place at Pabna Police Lines resulting in strong punitive action. Constables were paid Rs. 16 on first appointment in 1930. Three years' service would bring the amount to Rs. 17, after seven years of service, a constable would get Rs. 18, Rs. 19 after putting in ten years of service. After putting in seventeen years of service, a constable would receive a pay of Rs. 20. Constables submitted petitions individually for rise in pay. The burden of the petitions were the same; rise in price of essentials has led the petitioner to seriously think if he would continue to serve or go back home. The monthly expenditure shown after a constable in 1930 may be of some interest-as gleaned from a petition submitted from Tippera district. Charges were calculated on daily requirements.

Rice $\frac{1}{2}$ seer	-/2/-	Dal 3 Ch.	-/1/-
Aata $\frac{1}{2}$ seer	-/2/-	Oil 1 Ch.	-/-/9
Ghee 1 Chhatak	-/3/6	Condiment	-/-/6
Vegetables	-/1/-	Kerosene	-/-/6
Meat 2 Chhatak	-/1/6	Dry Wood	-/1/6
Fish	-/1/6	Milk 1 seer	-/4/-
	Total	Rs. 1/3/9	

With the monthly charges for washerman at the rate of eight annas and barber at four annas, the monthly expenditure was calculated at Rs. 37/12/9 only. The request was to increase the pay to Rs. 55 a month. It may seem that rates of commodities were shown on the higher side though.

However, in Malda district, the unrest among policemen did not precipitate any trouble in the long run.

In the wake of the non-co-operation movement, Khadi had been introduced in the district. Congress propaganda reached the interior villages by March 1922. In some 'jatra' (open-air theatrical performances) national songs and patriotic songs were sung and discourses on Hindu-Muslilm amity, khadi, charka etc. were held. Volunteers were moving around to spread the ideas of Congress and to organise the peasants. Even on August 31, 1922, one Jadab Ali Biswas of Jangipur, Murshidabad while addressing a meeting at Malda, suggested that the people should learn the use of arms to drive out the English. Action was taken against the speaker. Such actions had to be taken by the administrtation in later years as well.

Chapter 4

Barind the Hotbed

The area lying to the east of the Mahananda is known as Barind. According to traditions, Mahananda river is the boundary between Rarh and Barendra. During the Mughals the area was thickly populated and prosperous. After the Capital was shifted to Murshidabad and the decay of Gaur, Barind must have been depopulated and overgrown with jungles. By the time of the revenue survey, most of the northern parts, including Habibpur and Bamangola Police Stations was covered with dense forest and jungle; the southern portion was, however, under cultivation. The characteristic undulating ground of Barind stretches into Dinajpur and Rajshahi. As Mr. Carter writes, "The country is high, open and undulating, seamed with smaller watercourses in the valleys, and practically devoid of shade except for the village sites and small patches of Sal forest here and there in Habibpur Police Station. The ground is baked hard as iron, drinking water is scarce..and as one moves across the country, the eye is met by a seemingly endless series of terraced slopes, devoid of any crop, and quivering under the heat of the sun. In autumn the same country is a green expanse of winter rice."[1]

Hunter who based his account on the Collector's report of 1870, writes,"on the higher ground which gradually slopes away from the rivers to the jungle of the interior, crops of Rabi or transplanted winter-rice are grown, and some efforts are being made to reclaim the borders of the jungle. But little progress, however, has been made, for the ravages of wild beasts of all kinds cause great devastation, and the population is both scanty and unprogressive. The remainder of this tract of country, down to the borders of the low-lying land along the rivers is entirely occupied with thorny tree jungle called

1. Carter, M.O.: Final Report on the Survey and Settlement Operations in the District of Malda, 1928-1935, p. 2.

Katal. There are no large forests, but a continuous spread of jungly swamp, broken in upon by narrow steep nalas, and very thinly inhabited. The whole of this tract is generally known as the katal, and it extends from the civil station to the north-east and the south-east as far as the borders of Dinajpur".

The attempts at reclamation were continued shortly afterwards, when Santals migrated from Bihar and settled in Barind. They cleared the jungle, terraced the slopes and made the land fit for cultivation of winter-rice. Today the whole tract is under cultivation with the exception of parts of the valleys down which flow the Tangan and the Punarbhava rivers. These valleys, or Dubas as they are called locally, are two to four miles in width. During the rains they are one unbroken sheet of water until November when the water subsides, and cultivation of Boro paddy and rabi crops can begin. Cultivation is extending in these valleys but portions are still covered with coarse grass, hijol trees and wild rose bushes.

The reclamation programme could not have been for Santals initially. The number of Santals in 1872 was 215 only while the number of Oraons was many times more. Santals came to Barind after 1871 in larger numbers.

Immigration of Santals in Malda district from Santal Parganas and other districts continued till 1921. The following figures will speak for themselves:-

Number of Santals by Census of -

1872	215
1881	1,734
1891	20,989
1901	52,126
1911	52,128
1921	73,351
1931	72,145

The diminution was caused by emigration of some Santal families to the Barind region of Dinajpur and Morang in

Nepal. Immigration into Malda virtually stopped after 1921 as the process of reclamation of the waste lands of Barind was almost complete and the landlords had ceased to grant favourable terms to the Santals.

The following is a statement of land in Malda expressed in terms of percentage, during 1928-35.[2] Percentage of area cultivated to total land area-73.3. Percentage of area culturable but not cultivated to total land area-16.4. Percentage of area unculturable to total land area-10.3. Percentage of area cultivated to total culturable area-82.0.

Barind comprised of five police stations :Gazole, Bamongola, Habibpur, Nachole and Gomastapur. Police Stations Nachole and Gomastapur are presently in Bangladesh. Part of police station Malda responds to similar geophysical description and the Santal population in the jurisdiction is considerable. The mufassil areas are fairly inaccessible during the rains.

The distribution of Santal population in Barind was as folows:-

Gazol	22,640
Bamangola	8,543
Malda	7,879
Habibpur	23,715
Nawabganj	884
Nachole	3,397
Gomostapur	6,293
	Total : 73,351 (1921 Census)

Owing to preachings of the Christian Missionaries, about a thousand Santals had been converted into Christians within the fourth decade of the twentieth Century. During the same period, about thirtyeight thousand Santals were converted into Hinduism. Shri K.C.Barman attributes half of these conversions to Hinduism to Shri Kashiswar Chakraborty (a retired

2. Mitra, A: District Handbooks—Malda: Census 1951, Appendix II.

pleader of Dinajpur). The census figures would clearly reveal the position thus:

Figures of 1921 census-		
Hindu		678
Tribal (animists)		71,462
Christian		—
	Total	72,140
Figures of 1931 Census-		
Hindu		38,309
Tribal(animists)		32,879
Christian		957

The most striking feature of the earlier period is the rapid increases in population in the western side of the district, in thanas Ratua, Kaliachak and Shibgunj, and in the Barind on the east, in thanas Malda, Gazole, Gomastapur and Nawabgunj. This was due-in the former case to immigration, chiefly of Muhammadans from Murshidabad district, and in the latter case, to the influx of the Santals into Barind from the Santal Parganas. Between 1881 and 1890, nearly twenty thousand Santals and sixteen thousand Muhammadans from Murshidabad, had taken up land in the district. The Santals were attracted by jungle, which at that time covered much of the Barind, and by the low rates of rents which were offered to them for clearing it. In the next decade the colonisation of Barind reached its height. There was a tremendous influx of Santals and their population was returned in 1901 as fiftytwo thousand, compared with twenty-one thousand of the previous census. The following decade saw a further increase of over foruteen thousand, but thereafter the movement died away, and the Santal population remained more or less constant, immigration being balanced by migration to the Barind of Dinajpur and Rajshahi, and even to the Nepal Terai. The Muhammadan inflow continued steadily upto 1911 census. The Ganges had been moving westward and southward at the expense of Murshidabad, and the alluvial formation on the Malda side attracted large number of settlers who gradually spread inland. The general decrease shown by 1921 census was due to malaria, which broke out in epidemic form during several years and was particularly severe in the central part of the district.

It is significant to note that in the 1872 census the Hindus were the majority in the district: in that of 1931 they were a minority. The comparative figures are:

	1872	1931
Hindu	356298 = 52.7%	444406 = 42.2%
Muslim	310890 = 46.0%	571943 = 54.3%
Others	9238 = 1.3%	37417 = 3.5%

The large increase in the Muhammadan community was due primarily to the immigration from Murshidabad district, but also for higher birth rate. The increase under the head 'others' was due to the Santal influx in the Barind and a few thousand Oraons. It may be mentioned in passing that in the census of 1931, almost half of the Santal population was shown as Hindu. The Santals and Oraons, Hindus and animists taken together, formed about 7.5 per cent of the district population.

Orans believed the census figures on Hindu religious identification to be largely an artifice of census methods, and since at least the 1920's, often of coercian as well. He quoted Culshaw as follows:

"The prevailing Indian identification of race with religion has caused some confusion in their (the Santals') minds, but the fact that about 50 per cent of Santals were returned in 1931 as Hindus and most of the remainder as followers of tribal religion indicated the heightened political consciousness of the enumerators more that any real division within the tribe[3].

There is no denying the fact that the nationalist movement since 1920 had served to heighten the political consciousness of Indians in general. At the same time, the Santals in Barind had availed of the religious cover in propagating their ideas

---

3. Orans, Martin, The Santal: A Tribe in Search of a Great Tradition

simultaneously with the national movement. As restraining orders u/s. 144 Cr.P.C. were issued against holding political meetings, the impediment was circumvented by resorting to religious rites like worshipping the Kali, and the daily religious recitations. While Culshaw's remarks were pertaining to the district of Bankura, in Malda district- as the comtemporary report of K.C. Barman indicated, conversion to Hinduism was a real force under the leadership of Kashiswar Chakraborty and Jitu.

Muhammadans

Momin Jolah

Sk. Momin	6971
Sayyad	2049
Others	562923

Aboriginals

Santals	32879

Among the aboriginal classes, or classes which are of aboriginal origin, the Santals number thirtytwo thousand, Turis over four thousand, Koras and Oraons about three thousand, followed by Mundas and others.

Among the Hindus:-

Brahman	10000 (approx)
Kayasthas	3822 (approx)
Baidyas	671 (approx)
Hindu Santals	38309
Tantis	16000
Goalas and Nagars	14000 each
Binds and Tiyars	10000 each

The Santals came next to the Muslims as the agricultural community in the district. They were divided in four sects- the Christians, the Satyam Shibam, the Kharwars and the animists who retained all the aboriginal customs.

The Christians were comparatively few in number, and were converted to Christianity by the Protestant and the Catholic missionaries working in the district for the preceding two decades. The Roman Catholic Mission had a centre at Rohanpur and several churches in Barind. The missionaries were the first to introduce some sort of education to the Santals in small schools. It has to be recognised that the missionaries had stood by the Santals, may be converts, to protect them from the oppression from landlords and the money-lenders.

Opinions differ as to the time of origin of the Satyam Shibam Sect. J.N. Sengupta mentions the time as 1905 in the District Gazetteer edited by him in 1969. From the reckoning of M.O. Carter, the sect was founded in or about 1917. We shall find out later that around 1917 Jitu had been converted into Hinduism. The founder of the sect was Kashiswar Chakraborty, a pleader from Dinajpur. Both J.N. Sengupta and Carter mentioned in passing the motive of the founder being financial gain in part, and another aspect of the establishment of the sect was to bring the Santals in Hindu fold in the line of Arya Samaj. He made a deep impression on the Santals and a large number of them embraced Hinduism. They gave up eating pigs, fowls and other food considered obnoxious by the Hindus. In marriage and social customs they retained the tribal customs, though slightly mellowed by considerations for the women folk. Their moral and material condition did not improve by their conversion. Carter wondered why the founder picked up "Satyam Shibam" as the motto of the sect. "Satyam Shibam Sundaram is one used by the Brahmos but it is not clear why it was adopted by the reformer. Left to themselves, the Santals are naturally very much more truthful than most of their neighbours"[4]. Or, could it be a derivative from the 'Sari' Dharam of the tribals, which was propounded under the Sari Sarjom tree. Sari stands for truth, i.e., Satyam. Mythological parallels to Shiba had been drawn to convince the tribals of the basic unity of the two pantheons.

In another contemporary document, mention has been made of the amount that passed hands at the time of conversion.

---

4. Carter, M.O. : p.40

Under the leadership of Jitu, a considerable number of Santals became Hindus. Each convert had to pay 3-4-0 (rupee's three and four annas) for such conversion. These new converts in Hinduism had been assured of a high position in the Hindu caste system. Even though the promise was illusory, the new converts were very aggressive and stood against the rest.

There is no doubt that Kashiswar Chakraborty had his fees from the poor Santals for conversion. At a time when the annual rent for one bigha of land was six annas, Rs.3/4/= was quite some money. That the total accummulation had added to the wealth of Kashiswar Chakraborty cannot be denied. But if we have a look at his qualifications there can be little doubt that he could have earned the same amount in his legal profession. He forsook a practice and spent enough time with his devotees who used to address him as Thakurbaba. Coming from Dinajpur to the Barind in those days took both time and energy. Whatever Kashiswar gave to the tribals was evidently much more than he had taken in terms of money. He had given an identity to an oppressed group of tribals at their time of need. The motto he used was not that of the Brahmos, nor did it have anything to do with the truthfulness of the Santals. In the second decade of the twentieth century, new lores were developing ascribing to Shiba the overlordship of the various autochthonous janajatis. By Satyam Shibam, the founder of the sect wanted to convey to the Santals that they happened to be an integral part of the Hindu society in so far as Shiba, a non-Aryan diety, was taken in the Aryan pantheon. Through parallel myths, a fusion in identities of the two communities was attempted by the founder. Allowing the new converts a higher status in the Hindu society could not be an Arya Samajist plan. The Arya Samaj provided a common stratum for all converts. Kashiswar Chakraborty had tried to establish contact with the Hindu Sabha much later in 1926. In a postcard written on Novermber 26, 1926, Shri Chakraborty wanted to know the rules and regulations of setting up a Hindu Sabha at Dinajpur. The letter was addressed to Shri Padmaraj Jain, of Hindu Relief Committee, at 160, Harrison Road, Calcutta. Shri Jain was Vice-President of Hindu Sabha at that time and an ardent Congress Worker. Kashiswar had already started converting the Santals to Hinduism from 1917, if not from 1905. By himself, he could not have ascribed a higher status in the Hindu social hierarchy for the Santal converts. The Hindu Mission, however, had done the same thing. It had inducted aborigine groups in the Hindu fold by allowing them status as Kshatriyas. Elsewhere in November 1922 Kedranath Chakraborty, Secretary of the Raiyats' Association, had been holding meetings in Srivordi and Islampur areas in Faridpur and Barisal at which he had been telling the Hadis that they were Kshatriyas, and inciting them to demand that they should be styled as such in all Zamindari documents. Kedarnath Charkaborty was not a religious preacher but political agitator. And the Hadis were not required to be converted. Kashiswar Chakraborty, the lone preacher, had perhaps to remain contented with projecting a hope of higher status. By converting the Santals to Hinduism, Kashiswar had brought out the society from the defensive shell whereupon it was possible to develop a programme. It also facilitated the Santals in acquainting themselves with the movements of Gandhiji which had also influenced the tribals enormously. Thus Kashiswar lifted up an oppressed tribal group which was searching for a way out of the woods.

The Kharwars were the followers of the Sapha Hor propounded by Bhagrit Baba of Santal Parganas. The Sapha Hor movement had branched off in sects; a preacher of the Babaji sect used to visit Barind at intervals of about a year. It may be mentioned that the Saphat Hor do not take flesh nor do they drink toddy or Pachwai. There was similarity in observances and tenets between the Sapha Hor and the Satyam Shibam. While the latter were full-fledged Hindus, the former were Santals and half way to Hinduism. They had adopted the principles of pollution and purification of the Hindus. Both these were religious movements, eventually slipping into the slot of political machination.

The Zamindars of Bengal did play a role in clearing the waste that formed so prominent a part in the rural landscape around 1800. This they accomplished mainly by extending inducements in the form of rent exemptions or nominal rents to the relatively wild tribes to settle and clear the waste. As soon as the land was reclaimed, the Zamindar found legal ways to oust these tenants and replace them with more skillful tenants who would pay more rents. In the Zamindars, Lord Cornwallis had seen a social specimen that might turn into an enterprising English landlord who would clear the country and establilsh prosperous cultivation if he was assured of the future that he would not be taxed out of existence. Under the new rules, the Zamindar received a property right that promised to be stable. At the same time, he remained a tax-collector as in the Mughal regime. By the terms of the Permanent Settlement, the government took nine-tenths of the revenue that the Zamindar received from his peasant tenants, leaving for the Zamindar the tenth portion for his trouble and responsibility. The Zamindar augmented his income through various abwabs or imposts on the tenants, which varied from place to place. Through his device, the Zamindar is said to have doubled his rates of rent betwen 1800 and 1850. Meanwhile, growing pressure on land increased the power of the Zamindar and he made the most out of the situation.

With the firm establishment of the British authority, land-price started moving up. The partial intrusion of the market and the rise in land values brought about a change in the attitude of the moneylender who is an important feature in the rural scene. He served as a crude balance wheel to even out periods of scarcity and prosperity. Except in cases of severe famine, the peasant, could go to the money lender for a loan of grain when his own supplies ran short. Secondly, he was the customary source of cash when the peasant needed money for taxes. Naturally he did not perform these tasks without profit to himself. Before the British appeared on the scene, the money lender generally sought the peasant's crop, not the land which was abundant and of little value without someone to cultivate it. This situation continued until well into the second half of the nineteenth century, that is, until land values began to rise and British protection of property through the courts ran throughout the country. At this point of time the money lender began to change his tactics and sought to gain possession of the land itself, still leaving the peasant on it to cultivate it for him and produce a steady income.

From the report of Carter, it is clear that the better-known landlords of the district did not reside therein. The Maharaja of Mymensingh, the Maharaja of Lalgola, Shri Shanti Sekhareswar Roy of Taherpur were non-residents. The proprietor of the largest estate, the Raja of Chanchal also was living in Calcutta mostly. Of the resident families, Shri Ram Kinkar Roy and Shri Mohini Mohan Misra of Harichandrapur were scions of old aristocratic families. However, their interest did not extend in the Barind. In Englishbazar, the most influential family was that of Rai Saheb Jadunandan Choudhury and his cousin Shri Ashutosh Choudhury. This family traces its history to the days when Tanda was the capital of Bengal in the middle of the 16th century. Eventually, they settled down at Englishbazar and profited greatly in trade on silk and banking. They had acted as banyans of the East India Company, and their commercial activities were extended as far as Patna and Mirzapur. In the first half of the 19th century they started buying zamindary property and gradually increased their estates in the district. They had large interest in the Barind.

The Zamindars of Bulbulchandi and Singabad came of a Bhuihar Brahman stock and were related to the Maharaja of Lalgola. They had sprawling interests in the Barind, and as would be evident later, the mismanagement of the estates had greatly increased the maladies of the tribals.

Among Muhammadans, Begum Saheba of Rohanpur, and Khan Bahadur Abul Hayat Khan Choudhuri of Kotwali, were prominent. The Kotwali Zamindar descended from an old Pathan family that emigrated in the district several centuries ago and received the estate as a reward for military service. The Kotwali estate was gradually being impoverished. Khan Saheb, a reputed hunter of his days, was lavish in spending and hospitality. The gomastas had their time mulcting money out of the poor raiyats, extending their hold over alienated land from the Santals. A very insignificant part of the collections would find its way to the landlord. Otherwise, the fortunes of the zamindary would not have dwindled. There was talk of the estate passing into the hands of the Court of wards which would have relieved Khan Saheb to a great extent. This estate had large interests in Barind. Khan Bahadur received his titles during the civil disobedience movement for his loyal services.

Mention may also be made of the Khan Zamindars of Noorpur, another old Pathan family. The family had become impoverished. The Noorpur family, however, had no interest in Barind.

Two other families having large interests in Barind on account of their estates having landed property there, were the Shah Zamindars of Porsha and the Nandi Zamindars of Baidyapur, Burdwan. They had their Kutcheries and farm-houses and depended mostly on their agents.

Usually the big landlords had managers to look after the estate. The head office or sadar kutchery was generally in the village where the landlord lived. In outlying and convenient places tehsil kucheries were under charge of gomastas or agents. Naibs were placed over a few tehsil kutcheries. Various sections in the sadar kutchery were placed under charge of clerks. In the jama or account section mutations, settlements, accounts and annual audit were dealt. This section also looked after the collections in the tehsil kutcheries, and remittances. The karcha or the general register of tenancies was opened — a new every year, one page marked for each tenant. Daily transactions were noted along with number and year of rent receipts. A complete statement was to be prepared annually, basing on the karcha, showing each tenancy's accounts. The mufassil tehsildars used to submit statements alongwith counterfoils of rent receipt, unused receipt forms and daily cash book. The jarip or survey section dealt with maps, chittas, rent-rolls, Khatians, measurements, reports on mutation, settlements, encroachments, alluvion, diluvion and connected matters. The law section was concerned with filing, conducting and settling of suits, including the execution of decrees. Correspondence was dealt by the Munshikhana. Daily cash book, jama-kharch and annual returns were dealt by the Sumar or Cashier. The Mahafezkhana was the record room.

In well-managed estates things were in orderly fashion. An annual audit of collection and remittances would be done in all estates to the Sadar office in presence of tehsildars before orders for collection for the new year were issued.

The tehsil Kutcheries were run by gomasta or in big areas, by naibs, with assistance of muhurics, peons and sometimes a guard with the additional work of a menial. The tehsil Kutcheries maintained the rent receipts, Jamawashil Baki, Karcha, Rokar (or cash book), Bakijai (arrear list) and Amdani (daily cash book).

The percentage cost of estate management was found to be higher than that of government management. Carter reckoned the standard of work of these people to be inferior to government tehsildars.

The relation between the landlords and the tenants was strained. In view of that James Peddie proposed that the Settlement Operations should commence in Malda before schedule as otherwise the agrarian trouble might have intensified. The Settlement Operations were started later for Malda, but the request of the collector was acceded to and the operations started in 1928.

The landlords, as a class, depended entirely on their agents. They did never evince any interest in the economic welfare of their tenants, nor did they concern thesmelves with the agricultural improvements. The principal causes of ill-feeling between the landlords and tenants were exactions of various abwabs, the illegal enhancements of rent, non-grantal of rent receipts, the levy of interest at high rates, and the rapacity and oppression of the landlords 'agents, gomastas and peadas. In the year following the commencement of the Settlement Operations, the agricultural produces did not fetch enough price due to economic depression. The tenants were in difficulty to make payment of rents; the landlords were sceptical and thought the tenants were deliberately trying to avoid payment using the depression as a pretext. It may also be recalled that the drought of 1928 led to the elevation and improvement of the road from Bulbulchand to Nala through test relief costing about fifty thousand rupees in the Barind.

Abwabs at varying rates were imposed by all estates. It was estimated that the total amount realised as abwabs would not be less than the total land-revenue of the district. Barring a few cases, abwabs generally went in the pockets of the gomastas. Carter has left an illuminating record of these abwabs prevailing at the time of the Settlement Operations. Tohuri, the "perquisite of the gomasta or naib, amounted not less than two annas in a rupee; and the peadagan, the perquisites of the underlings of the naib, to one anna. In many estates one anna was also realised as the cost of rent receipt, and various levies were made on account of social or religious ceremonies. Some estates realised the cost of their rent collecting agency; one estate levied a tax when marriage ceremonies took place in a tenant's house, the rate being Rs. 5/- for a son and Rs. 2/8/ for a daughter. The Harischandrapur Zamindars realised one anna in the rupee as a contribution to their dramatic club, and the Chowdhury estate in Englishbazar collected a tax in Gazole Police Station on each plough. Some estates realised abwabs in the name of deities, but appropriated the major portion themselves; and most estates made special levies on the occasion of various ceremonies in the landlord's house, such as marriages or Sradh ceremonies, or for the purchase of a motor car, an elephant, or a gun. The Chanchal estate, which was one of the better managed zamindaries, realised 'tohuri' at one anna in the rupee and the tenants did not complain against payment. Generally speaking, there was little or no complaint against the imposition of small abwabs; it was only when the landlord's agents became too greedy that the tenants complained, and in Malda their rapacity in some estates was perhaps unequalled"[5].

---

5. Carter. M.O. : p. 96

Realisation of the illegality of abwabs did not deter the tenants from paying up, as that would have invited more trouble for them. Carter suggested that the Collector should be empowered to look into the matter of abwabs, rather than the civil courts. He also suggested strong law on the score. Another feature having undesirable effect on the system was the systematic underpayment to the zamindari staff. Except Chanchal estate, the pay of gomastas/naibs varied between rupees five and ten a month, with the privilege of fending for themselves.

Abwabs were realised in all the estates in Bengal, though at varying rates. Raiyat associations or Sabhas in almost all the districts were vociferous against the illegality of those exactions and sought to put a stop to the malady by inciting the raiyats not to pay at all. The exhortations were on the increase in the wake of the non-cooperation and Khilafat movements. In July 1922 Raiyat Sabha was held in Murshidabad, organised by Maulavi Messer Ali of Murshidabad, urging raiyats not to pay any abwabs to the Zamindars. Similar meetings had taken place earlier in most of the districts.

Abwabs were universal in nature, but the rates were higher in Barind. Ignorance of the tenants facilitated the realisation. In many cases the tenants, particularly the Santals, did not even know the actual rent they were supposed to pay; the amount realised as abwab was totalled with the rent and the reckoning was on the total amount paid. Carter's estimate was that a Santal paid at least 1/3rd of his legal rent in additional abwabs. There was no remedy whatever against the state of affairs except altering the law. The custom of paying abwab was stronger than the law which forbade it. And for obvious reasons, the tenants never felt like taking the line of confrontation with the landlords, for the meagre prospect of inconsequential penalty to the landlord at Court for infringement of section 75 Bengal Tenancy Act. A list of abwabs realised by various estates is quoted below from Carter's report.

Thana	*Estates*	*Abwabs*
Habibpur	Porsha Shahs ...	As. 8 in the rupee
	Harihar Satiar ...	As. 12 in the rupee
	Bulbuli Singabad	On the average As. 4 in the rupee. The tenants had to pay between Re. 1 and Rs. 2 to see the landlord.
Gazole	Rai Sahib J.N. Chowdhury	The average abwab was over As. 4 in the rupee.
	Girija Kanta Das The Sanyyals	Tahsildars were either not paid or were paid a nominal amount, and make the rest out of the tenants. Rai Sahib H.N. Choudhury levied a tax on each plough.
Old Malda	Girija Kanta Das and others	The abwabs varied from As. 4 to As. 8 per rupee Fees for Tahasildars and peons, the cost of establishment, the cost of rent receipts and subscriptions to various festivities were realised. On the average a tenant paid as abwabs not less than 1/3rd. of the legal rent.
Gomastapur	Taherpur estate (Sasi Sekhareswar Roy) Brojendra MaitraBegum Saheba of Rohanpur.	The general rate of abwab varied from As. 2 to As. 8 per rupee. Interest on arrear rents was charged at 25 per cent. The abwab in the Begum Saheba estate was As. 3-9 which is fairly moderate for the Barind.[6]

6. Carter M.O. : p. 83

Illegal enhancements of rent were the order of the day. The usual practice was to carry out an estate survey to reduce the existing standard of measurement and to assess rent at the same or slightly increased rate. For instance in the estate survey a bigha would be measuring 80 x 80 cubits, whereas the earlier measurement had been 90 x 90 cubits; thus increasing the plot under survey in area on paper though the tenant did not actually get any increase. The same result might be obtained by altering the lengths of the cubits. In some estates, the cubit measured 18 inches, but by adopting the cubit equivalent of 16 inches would effect an increase in area on paper. Chanchal estate derived benefits this way in 1904 and the increase in rent amounted to eight annas a rupee. The Talanda estate in Gomastapur and Nachole Thanas was surveyed in 1917, excess rent was demanded for the excess area, and an illegal enhancement was made. In the absence of any registered Kabuliyats, there was no proof that the original settlement of rent was based on an area found after survey, and the enhancement was cut down under Section 29 Bengal Tenancy Act, as it was in excess of the allowable limit. A concerted movement resulted out of the problem, leading to stoppage of paying taxes, and the tenants availed of the opportunity of the attestation work in 1931-32. The Monakosha estate owned by Moulvi Jahur Ahmed Chowdhury was surveyed and effected an enhancement in 1931 which was resisted by the tenants. News of oppression and torture on the tenants by the landlord's agents reached the district administration and the Moulvi had to be advised sternly. The Taherpur estate of Shri Sasi Sekhareswar Roy caused illegal enhancements by circumventing the provisions of Section 29 Bengal Tenancy Act by amalgamation or splitting up of tenancies. Two enhancements were made in twenty years, but the landlords safeguarded themselves by taking kabuliyats. Many holdings which had been made khas by rent sales were lying uncultivated. Deeply aggrieved at the attitude of the landlords on the question of enhancement of rent, the tenants socially boycotted the estate employees in Gomastapur and Nachole thanas for about six months.

In most estates rent receipts were not properly issued. The most common form of illegalilty was to accept part payment of rent and to refuse rent receipt till full payment was made. Even if payments were made, along with abwabs frequently rent receipts would be issued after a few days. The tenants seldom raised questions. Fines were imposed on the Singabad and Bulbuli Zamindars under Section 58 Bengal Tenancy Act, but the situation hardly registered any improvement. The rent receipts suffered from other irregularities like not mentioning the area, nor showing the year for which payment was made. This was aimed at realising arrears having long been time-barred in some estates, particularly the Bulbuli estate, as such estates continued to carry over such unrealised rents in registers. The Bulbuli estate had claimed enhancements which were denied by the tenants. The unpaid enhancements were entered as 'arrears' in the estate accounts for many years, interest was charged on it and consequently it was not uncommon to find a tenant with an annual rental of Rs. 5/- showing an outstanding rent to the tune of rupees two thousand. As such, it was not possible for the tenant to know which year the payment had been credited to. The system allowed the landlord to credit all payments to the oldest arrears, keeping a holding perpetually in arrears of rent and liable to be sold away at any moment.

The Bulbuli estate was also guilty of the deliberate destruction of rent receipts, obtained from tenants on various pretexts. Rev. Cattaneo of Rohanpur had brought up several such cases before Carter.

Some other oppressive practices strained the relation between the landlords and the tenants. One of the most common practices in the Barind was to increase the area of the Kamat or farm of the landlord, at the cost of the tenant, adding forcibly land from the tenants' holding. Needless to say, the tenant would have to pay the same rent-no corresponding reduction in rent would be effected. The Shah Zamindars or Porsha conceived an innovation to cheat the tenants by taking away the tenants' rights by bogus settlements with various relations, and issuing rent receipts to the tenants in which they were shown as under-raiyats. When the relationship between the landlord and the relatives was examined, the fraud was exposed. It was found out that no rent was actually paid and that there was no relationship existing. This had happened in Habibpur thana. In the same thana, the Ejmali estates-those of Bulbuli and Singabad were realising the full rent of holdings instead of part rent according to their shares. These estates were partitioned amicably on the basis of the record of rights. Many landlords in Barind distrained the crops of their tenants, though formal complaints hardly came to the administration. 'Begar'or forced labour was also in vogue in Barind where the tenants seemed to be under the impression that they were legally bound to submit to it. Even during the days of Carter, the tenants in Barind used to work at their landlords' houses on festive occasions, and in some estates they were required to cultivate the landlords khamar land.

Oppression and malpractices described above were present in a very pronounced manner in Barind where almost all the Santal population of the district resided. Their ignorance, improvidence and illiteracy made them easy prey for the landlords' unscrupulous agents and the money-lenders. The attitude of the Hindus in the neighbourhood to the Santals was a contemptuous sufferance, and for cheating a poor Santal nobody had ever been assailed by moral qualms. The easiest way to dispossess the Santal of his holding was to go to the civil court, suppress the processes and obtain an ex-parte decree. Carter mentioned a case where a Santal had actually lost his holding because he had borrowed some salt from his mahajan. Instances of deliberate cheating were also in galore. A 'Khot Kobala' is a form of mortgage. By substituting the word 'Khos' for 'Khot' ir a mortgage deed, the transaction would become an outright sale. Land involved in such transactions as took place before the application of Chapter VIIA to Malda district could not be given back to the tribals. The total effect of rapacity, indifference and exactions had disastrous effect on the Santals in Barind. According to the estimate of Carter, at least in 25000 acres, the Santals had lost their occupancy rights. The chart showing the alienation of land, thana-wise, is quoted from the report of Carter.[7]

Thana	*Area (Sq.Miles)*	*Area expropriated (Sq.miles)*	*Area expropriated from aboriginals*
Bamongola	69.32	1.46	1.10
Habibpur	156.73	9.00	6.75
Gazole	196.84	6.36	4.77
Malda	87.15	8.10	6.08
Gomastapur	122.64	20.34	10.17
Nachole	109.70	10.53	5.27
Nawabganj	55.90	9.00	4.50
Total:	798.28	64.77	38.64

It is not that the Zamindars had all along gained by land-alienation from the tribals. In many cases gomastas misappropriated the land if the landlord was not wary enough. The motivating factor was to augment income by such exactions. The low salary of the gomastas has been mentioned before, and the incentive was the scope of earning through such practices as mentioned. We may mention a gomasta of the Kotwali estate whose monthly salary was Rs. 9/-only. This gomasta had acquired about four mouzas of land-all expropriated from the tribals, which fact was not known to the landlord. Later, the incumbent had to disgorge all the land that he had swallowed at the instance of the Special Officer, Barind. At the latter's request, the landlord, however, raised his monthly pay to Rs. 25/-

Another case of land-alienation had come to the notice of the administration, and the Special Officer, Barind set it right by restoring the land to the original owner. The tribal was

7. Carter, M.O. : p. 83

advised by the gomasta that he owed the Zamindar fifteen rupees by way of arrear taxes. Not being able to pay forthwith,the tribal prayed for time. In consideration of a turban of mulmul, worth five annas, the gomasta agreed to receive payment of arrear rents in weekly instalments of three annas on the weekly market-day. The Santal bought the turban on loan from the shop of a mahajan, and continued to pay rent as agreed to the gomasta. After about seven years, the tribal was dispossessed of his holding of seven bighas by a decree of the Civil Court for an accumulated loan of Rs. 200/- this land was taken over by the mahajan himself.

Chapter VIIA Bengal Tenancy Act was extended to the Santals of Malda in 1923, and to the Oraons in 1927. Under its provisions, no aboriginal could sell or mortgage his land without written permission from the Collector. This enabled the Collector to look into each such case. Unfortunately, law did not empower the Collector to impose his decision on the money-lender who squarely refused to advance money in many cases. In usufructuary mortgage also, the position of the Collector was at best recommendatory; the money lender walked out in most cases refusing to advance the loan. To ameliorate, it was felt that a bank to provide loans to tribals should be set up. Later, a proposal was sent to the government without any result.

Village Audhua in Gazole PS was inhabited by Santals, Turis, Chitrakars and Deshis. In November 1913 a quarrel broke out between Shibu Mandal, Nikhil Deshi, Bara Ramray Santal and others of Audhua forming the first party, and Sk. Sadagar Mia, Hazi Maniruddin and others of Sahapur, PS Malda forming the second party, over possession of land measuring about 200 bighas. Police submitted report to the Court so that both the sides be restrained from entering the land. The Court ultimately decided the matter in favour of the second party on 13.1.1914. In the dispute, two landlords were behind the scene-Krishna Jiban Sanyal of Kansat was helping the first party while the second party was helped by Ambika Charan Nundy of Baidyapur, Burdwan district.

Troubles over land do take place now-a-days even. But in those days, it was always the Santal who lost in land or freedom; for they did not know the implications of law and legal orders, nor did they understand the implications of not attending the court on dates fixed.

In another case, a dispute over possession over 16 bighas of land between Dipchand Mandal and Birjoo Santal of Saroadal in Gazole PS was settled by the Magistrate in favour of Birjoo in November 1917. In February 1918, Panchanan Mandal (Dipchand's son) picked up Chhatku Santal as his victim and prayed to the Court for restraining Chhatku from entering into a particular plot of land. Chhatku did not appear on the date—there was nothing to indicate that notices were ever received by Chhatku-so an order under Section 144 Cr.P.C. was made absolute ex-parte. In November 1918, there was a riot when Panchanan came to harvest the paddy from that plot of land. Birjoo Santal and his kins were sentenced to undergo six months' rigorous imprisonment for injuring Panchanan Mandal by arrow-shots.

One Jahurmull Sett of Malda purchased a plot of land measuring about 4 bighas, from Satish Chandra Chakraborty of Ranaghat who purchased the same from Sujan Santal of Haldibari long back. Jahurmull Sett made adhi-bandobast (share-cropping) with some tenants. Sidho Santal, brother of Sujan Santal claimed this land and opposed the new purchaser from harvesting the standing paddy crops. Jahurmull thereafter filed a petition to the Court. Police made inquiry and submitted report to the Court, requesting for an order to restrain the poor Santal from entering into the plot of land. Court obliged and an injunction was issued restraining Sidho Santal, Chhotka Santal, Sufal Santal, Kaloo Santal, Hopa Santal, all of Haldibari and Bipin Rajak of Fulbari in Englishbazar Police Station. Police executed the order. The land was lost to the Santal. During the whole process nobody looked into the matter to ascertain how Satish Chandra Chakraborty, a Hindu Brahman could purchase land from Sujan Santal, a tribal.

Gandhu Santal and his father Salkhan Santal of village Babudanga were convicted for six months rigorous imprisonment for 'looting' standing paddy from a plot of land which the convicted persons thought to be theirs. Bhupendra Nath Chakraborty of Old Malda had started a case direct at the Court alleging that his share-croppers had cultivated the plot. When the crop was ripe, Gandhu and his father sought to seize the same on the presumption that they were the actual owners of the land. From the Court, an order under Section 144 Cr. P.C. was issued, but the Santals had reaped the harvest before it was promulgated. Nevertheless, the Santals were sentenced to jail. Nobody probed how a plot of land could be claimed simultaneously by a Hindu Brahman and a Santal tribal.

Shri K.C. Barman mentioned more glaring cases of cheating the Santals of land in his report. "A Santal had to lose 15 bighas of land for purchasing a dietz lantern on credit. Another borrowed Rs. 25 in 1925, and in 1928 paid back Rs. 26, and in 1930 Rs. 45. But this year the mahajan has obtained against him a decree from the civil court of Nawabganj for Rs. 195 plus costs".[8]

The trouble between the Santals and their landlords began around 1907 at Gazole when they resorted to 'no tax' movement in protest against illegal enhancement of rent. This trouble was short-lived. In 1910, when the landlords of Touzis No. 586 and 587 in Habibpur thana sought to enforce an enhancement of rent, the Santals made a representation to the government, alleging oppression and unfair exactions by the gomastas and peadas. Mr. Vas, the then Collector was appointed arbitrator, and was accepted by both the sides. The landlords had induced the Santals to migrate from the Santal Parganas and further west, and after the jungle in the Barind had been cleared, the slopes terraced, the landlord wanted an enhancement. The Santals were holding the land they cleared at nominal rents, or rent-free. As a result of Mr. Vas's settlement, the lands were measured-though no map was prepared-and the rent was fixed at six annas a bigha; provision was made for payment of arrear rent. The Santals stood by

8. Barman, K.C: Report on the condition of the Santhals in Malda, 1934, p. 18

this settlement all along and resisted any attempt of enhancement of rent by the landlords. The attempts to enhance rent was a constant irritant to the Santals.

The Civil Courts did nothing to improve the situation. Rather, the unscrupulous persons availed of the mechanism in obtaining ex-parte decrees against tribals particularly whose utter ignorance about law and procedure made the situation worse confounded. Carter quotes from the Circle Notes of Habibpur and Malda Thana, thus:

'In due course the mortgage is foreclose, in the majority of cases suppressing the notice, and property sold only to be purchased by Mahajans'. The tenants in happy ignorance continue to till the land for sometime, when Mahajan takes mutation from the landlord, and proceeds to possess the land'[9]

Cases were found where rent was paid but not credited to the accounts. Suits were instituted, notices were suppressed and the land was ultimately sold. The tehsildar did this in collusion with others to purchase the land in auction. The suppression of notices could never be proved anyway. The Santal, being too poor and ignorant of the procedure would not know to seek readress against such ex-parte orders. As a result, the executive authority of the district was forced to support the authority of the Civil Court against a Santal with whom his sympathy lay.

Carter mentioned the case of a Santal whose holding was sold out in the Sessions Court without his knowledge. When the purchaser came to take possession of the land, the Santal defended his right and went to the extent of shooting an arrow at the man who eventually died. The Santal was sentenced to seven years' rigorous imprisonment. Though he had exceeded his right of private defence, he could not prove that the holding was sold out without his knowledge and by suppressing the sale notices. On the evidence, the legal presumption was

9. Carter, M.O. : p.84

otherwise. Even administrators of the day were strongly against the Civil Courts dealing with suits against Santals. The large number of ex-parte decrees was indicative of either suppression of notices or perfunctory execution of the same. The following figures obtained from the Civil Courts pertaining to the period from 1928 to 1933 have been cited by Carter:

Rent Suits—

Cases heard ex-parte	:	881
Percentage	:	88

Mortgage Suits—

Cases heard ex-parte	:	172
Percentage	:	82

Though creation of a non-regulation district was not favoured by Carter, yet he felt that the work of dealing with civil suits involving Santals should be given over to the Executive Magistrate.

Three statements as recorded in Shri K.C.Barman's report would project a clearer picture in respect of the working of the Civil Court.

"Statement showing the number of rent suits instituted against the Santhals and Oraons of this district during the last five years with the terms of their disposal.

Name of Court	*Year*	*Total No. of Suits.*	*Terms of disposal*				*Remarks*
			Ex-parte	*On contest*	*Compro-mise*	*Dismissed*	
Ist Court	1932-33	123	105	1	14	3	
	1931-32	93	78	8	5	2*	*With-drawn
	1930-31	51	47	—	—	4	
	1929-30	225	198	3	—	24	
	1928-29	48	40	—	1	7	
	Total	540	468	12	20	40	

Name of Court	Year	Total No. of Suits.	Terms of disposal				Remarks
			Ex-parte	On contest	Compro-mise	Dismissed	
2nd Court	1932-33	145	128	1	14	2	
	1931-32	140	122	14	2	2	
	1930-31	78	68	1	2	7	
	1929-30	56	41	8	5	2	
	1928-29	58	54	3	1	—	
	Total	477	413	27	24	13	
	Grand Total	1017	881	39	44	53	

Ex-parte rent suits 88 per cent

Statement showing the number of money-suits on simple bond or hatchittas instituted against the Santals and Oraons of this district during the last five years with terms of their disposal.

Name of Court	Year	Total No. of Suits.	Terms of disposal				Remarks
			Ex-parte	On contest	Compro-mise	Dismissed	
Ist Court	1932-33	22	17	3	1	1	
	1931-32	50	38	3	9	—	
	1930-31	64	42	2	10	10	
	1929-30	30	15	2	9	4	
	1928-29	32	22	1	3	6	
	Total	198	134	11	32	21	
2nd Court	1932-33	24	18	3	2	1	
	1931-32	—	—	—	—	—	

Name of Court	*Year*	*Total No. of Suits.*	*Terms of disposal*				*Remarks*
			Ex-parte	*On contest*	*Compro-mise*	*Dismissed*	
	1930-31	—	—	—	—	—	
	1929-30	44	24	4	3	13	
	1928-29	13	6	—	—	7	
	Total	81	48	7	5	21	
	Grand Total	279	182	18	37	42	

Ex-parte money suits on simple bond 65.3 per cent

Statement showing the number of suits for recovery of sums secured by mortgage deeds instiuted against the Santals and Oraons of this district during the last five years with the terms of their disposal.

Name of Court	*Year*	*Total No. of Suits.*	*Terms of disposal*				*Remarks*
			Ex-parte	*On contest*	*Compro-mise*	*Dismissed*	
Ist Court	1932-33	8	8	—	—	—	
	1931-32	9	7	—	2	—	
	1930-31	6	5	1	—	—	
	1929-30	12	9	3	—	—	
	1928-29	21	19	—	2	—	
	Total	56	48	4	4	—	
2nd Court	1932-33	5	3	—	2	—	
	1931-32	11	10	—	1	—	
	1930-31	3	2	—	1	—	

Name of Court	Year	Total No. of Suits.	Terms of disposal				Remarks
			Ex-parte	On contest	Compro-mise	Dismissed	
	1929-30	9	7	1	1	—	
	1928-29	4	2	1	—	1	
	Total	32	24	2	5	1	
	Grand Total	88	72	6	9	1	

Ex-parte money suits on mortgage deeds 82 per cent.[10]

Even in 1934, K.C. Barman commented that the trend of land-alienation still persisted, and that there was extreme necessity of arming the officials with legal powers to stop land-alienation from the Santals. In his reckoning, 20 per cent of the land belonging to Santals had been expropriated from the Santals over the years.

The Santal peasantry in Barind could never rise above the situation necessitating loans. The monocrop Barind did not help by way of yield. Diversification was not possible for want of irrigation facilities. Multiplicity of markets did not come as a panacea to the peasants. They were obliged to sell out to buy more urgent items for the household. As revenue demand fell heaviest immediately after the harvest, they needed a market near at hand; they did not have the cash-flow to meet their commitments while holding their crop for storage and transportation. The most important need was for credit to enable them to tide over crop failures, replenish their stock and seed, and to indulge in occasional but lavish expenditure on dowries and wedding feasts. Continuance of production from one cycle to another was not possible in most cases without recourse to outside sources of finance and credit. The Santal peasants of Barind had never been independent cultivators. They had all the constraints- small holdings, adverse effects of land tenure and the mechanics of agricultural production.

10. Barman, K.C. : pp. 23-24.

Chapter 5

Santals in Barind : Relation with the Administration

It has already been said that the main phalanx of Santals had come over to Barind after 1870. The number grew with the years and vast tracts of land in the Barind were given over to them by the Zamindars for cultivation, on nominal rent. The lands having been converted into agricultural holdings by terracing the slopes and clearing the forest and underbrush-particularly in the Katal area-the Zamindars saw it fit to raise land-taxes. A systematic attempt was at hand to displace the poor, illiterate Santals from the land they had cleared by their hard labour and sweat. The money-lenders, the agents of the landlords, and in quite some cases the landlords themselves, innovated various means whereby they would fleece the poor tribal-without any moral qualm. Around 1907, the Santals took a bold stand. There was an attempt by the Zamindars of Bulbulchandi, Singabad and Porsha (in Dinajpur) to increase land-taxes whereupon the Santals objected enmasse. A representation was sent to the government. In the dispute, Mr. Vas, the then Collector of Malda was accepted as a mediator by both the contending parties. The Santals held the administration in grave suspicion of colluding with the landlords. By persistent effort, Mr. Vas could effect a compromise between the landlords and the Santals, by giving a decision which was accepted by the Santals who have been adhering to that scheme. In the dispute centering round Pargana Shikarpur, the Santals submitted to the arbitration of Mr. C.B.Lambrerue, the succeeding Collector.

In fact, measures were under contemplation of the administration to safeguard the interests of the Santals. At times, administrators resorted to extra-legal methods even to help the tribals. Mr. James Peddie, Collector had the inevitable urge of tearing down the loan-papers and documents of the money-lenders whenever it related to the Santals; for, he had the conviction that the Santals were being wronged. But the legal flaws and leaks sunk the boat of benevolence. The Santals continued to lose their land, being steeped in debt. Naturally, they did not appreciate the role of the administration and failure was attributed to partisan attitude towards the landlords and money-lenders. There was no way of knowing even in 1910 that the Collectors were finding it difficult to plug the holes by means of the inadequate provisions of the Bengal Tenancy Act. A mist of distrust grew up between the two sides.

Another issue brought bitterness between the Santals and the administration. Over the years, there developed a custom whereby the Santals used to catch fish from beels or extensive water-logged areas. This might have started in Barind when the Santals opened up the jungle land for cultivation, with a low density of population. Gradually, Barind drew more men from the near about places who flocked there to thrive. The administration also saw it fit to lease out the beels to have more revenue. The Zamindars followed suit. The lease-holders wanted to restrain the Santals from fishing in the beels as a form of possession. The real loss out of such fish-catching was negligible, as the Santals did not run any business on the query; the catch was shared by all the tribals for consumption. The lease-holders were apprehensive that such privilege might be construed as a matter of right of use. They appealed to the administration. The Santals, on the other hand, were convinced that they had been following a traditional custom. Their ancestors had been doing so and they had cleared the jungle land and were having the privilege. So they went on catching fish, even though the lease-holders protested and the administration frowned. In this practice, other local ethnic groups like the Poli, Rajbanshi, Lohars, and Momins (many of whom were suspected Wahabis) had been lending hands. The district administration bound down some Santals under Section 107 Cr.P.C. and the Sessions Judge confirmed the proceedings. But that did not have any permanent effect on them.

In April 1923, more than a thousand Santals looted fish from the beels-jalkars of Zamindars- for which three cases were started against them. Twelve persons were convicted in those cases. Again, in November 1923, about 1000/1500 Santals of Gazole-Bamangola-Malda thanas and of Itahar and Banshihari thanas of Dinajpur district indiscriminately looted fish from certain beels in Gazole and Bamangola thanas. An armed force of one Head Constable and ten Constables was deputed by the administration on 20th November to March through the jalkars and principal Santal villages in Gazole PS in a bid to run fear through the populace.

The Santal volunteers of Malda district had been moving in the adjoining Santal-inhabited villages of Dinajpur district; the response there added to the anxiety of Dinajpur district authorities who took measures to explain the situation to the tribals of that district. In fact, communal fishing in beels and distribution of spoils among the participants themselves speak of the collective enterprise of the same order as hunt or fishing. The corporate violence was to undermine the authority of the enemy and the government.

Persistent efforts led to a solution of the fishing problem. It was agreed upon that the Santals would not fish in the beels before the Holi festival. The Santals kept their promise to the Collector, Mr. James Peddie and had been catching fish in a body only after the Holi festival when the beels dried up leaving very little fish in the shallow waters after being caught by the lease-holders. There was generally no objection from anybody except from the landlords of Singabad. Mr. Peddie left the district on 13.2.29. Later handbills were distributed asking the Santals not to indulge in this practice even after the Holi festival.

By 1921, the number of Santals in the Barind came to slightly more than 70,000. After Bankura, Midnapore and Dinajpur, Malda was having the largest settlements of Santals. They presented a serious problem to the administration and required special care of the Collector. During the non-cooperation days they were gained over by agitators and had since paid but a small proportion of the rents due to them and had, to some extent, become more temperate. The association of the Santals with some Momins (suspected to be Wahabis) was also looked upon with suspicion. The activities of the Momins were also subjected to unobstrusive watch. It was conceded that not all the Momins were Wahabis, but they were certainly in sympathy with them. In 1854-60, the Wahabis had raised a small rebellion in the district. The strife between the Wahabis and the Hanifis in Barind was also a matter of concern to the administration. In December 1923, there was a near tragedy when, after a religious disputation between the two, fifty Wahabis were beseized in a house and the Hanifis set fire to the house. One of the Wahabis fired at the Hanifis from his gun and scared them away. Later, the dispute was amicably settled.

Even then, the administrators were thinking what to do with the Santals. It was confirmed by all that the poor Santals were utterly fleeced by wily money lenders and landlords and their agents. Yet, the legal provisions to effect a cure was found inadequate. The extension of Section 49A of the Bengal Tenancy Act did not improve matters much; for, the money-lenders shrank from giving loans on the security of their land. It was felt that the government would have to come forward to give loans to the Santals. This was the observation of Mr. R.Douglas, Collector of Malda even in October 1924. This thought crystallised later in proposals for opening a loan Bank in the district for the Santals. But in the absence of any direct communication between the administration at an appropriate level, as in the Santal Parganas after the Santal Rebellion of 1855-56, the Santals of Barind read apathy in the administration. Meanwhile, they had already been irked by a series of civil and criminal cases in which they had been faring badly. In March 1924, a crowd of about two thousand Santals beseized a bevy of eight Constables in a hut until one of them fired from the musket and scared away the offenders. The mood of the Santals was really getting sullen and even in 1924 it was felt that the tribals would confront the administration one of these days with bows and arrows. Father Anselmo of

Rohanpur Mission Church (an Italian Mission) was trying his best to alleviate the tension as he was intensely interested in the Christian Santals of Barind. It may be mentioned that Father Cattaneo of the same church had displayed the same concern for the Santals, and was eventually nominated to the District Board to represent the interest of the Santals.

Over the years, the condition of the Santals deteriorated. The bad management of the Bulbuli and Singabad zamindaries worsened the condition. There was a partition suit between the two Zamindars. Tenants were harassed by settlement to different tenants on the same land. Paddy crop would be attached till tenants agreed to enhance rents. In the zamindari sheristha, registration would give rise to endless harassment and fleecing; and even after payment of money there would remain disputes over which the tenants had no control. The abwabs were increasing. One co-sharer would exact full rent and the other would sue the tenant. The district administration could not effect redress to the grievances of the tenants though it had been pressurising the Zamindars. The Porsha Zamindars and the Kotwali estate were also creating problems; the ill-paid agents were playing havoc in the mufassil kutcheries. In this backdrop, the Swarajists were making a move among the tribals. They won the hearts of the tribals by urging them to stop illegal abwabs to the Zamindars. Of course, this was a programme pursued by the non-cooperators throughout Bengal. In Malda, particularly in Barind, meetings of raiyats were being held. In March 1923, subscriptions were being raised from the raiyats to defray the expenses of a visit of Shri Kedar Nath Chakraborty, Secretary of the Raiyat Association. A meeting of the raiyats was held at Jagdalla in Bamangola thana on 18th March 1923, the object being to stop payment of miscellaneous demands to the Zamindars beyond the actual rent. About 1200 Santals attended. Mahendranath Chakraborty of Jagdalla, and Gopinath Das of Simla were urging the tenants of Jadunandan Chaudhuri to stop payment, in June 1923. Around November 1923, Santals were showing signs of restiveness. Sagiruddin Sarkar of Noapara in Bamangola thana had convened two meetings on 24th and 26th November 1923, where he urged the audience not to pay any abwab to the Zamindars. These meetings were largely attended by the Santals of Habibpur and Bamangola. In these meetings Sagiruddin and his followers realised subscription of one anna per bigha of land to cope with the Zamindars. The Santals caught the idea. Even in 1921 a nucleus of Santal leadership had already formed to take up cue in Barind. This association with the anti-government movements brought about more strain on the tie between the Santals and the administration. Another significant aspect was that there was no dialogue between the administration and the Santals. The repressive programmes of the then government made it difficult also. There was an attempt to make changes in the legal procedure so that the tribals would not have to go to the Civil Courts. The intention was that the Executive Magistrate of the District would listen to their grievances and dispense ready justice. But the change in the statute could not be effected. Nor could the administration save the Santals from the oppressive money-lenders and landlords. Rather, in assisting to carry out the decrees of the Civil Courts, the administration became more unpopular with the Santals who had not the ability to distinguish between the Civil Courts and the general administration.

On 21.7.32 one Saral Ram Saha of Balia Nawabganj in Malda thana filed a petition in the Court of the Sub-Divisional Officer to the effect that one Raban Santal of Chandandighi took a loan of Rs. 175/- by keeping a mortgage of 11 bighas and 14 cuttahs of land. When this Raban Santal could not at all clear up the loan within the time fixed, Saral Ram Saha got the land mortgaged on the execution of a decree and got the possession of the land by the authority of Court. Saral Ram Saha with his men came down to the land for cultivating the same. Raban Santal and his three sons namely; (1) Tulia Santal, (2) Mongal Santal and (3) Guhia Santal opposed them with bows and arrows. Consequently, a petition was forwarded by the S.D.O. to the thana for local enquiry and report. A local enquiry was made into the petition by A.S.I. A.Ahmed and the allegation was proved satisfactorily. Warning notices were issued on the Santals then and there at the spot and report was submitted praying for the issue of injuction notices under Section 144 Criminal Procedure on Raban Santal, Tulia Manjhi, Mongal Santal and Guhia Santal. The injunction notices were then issued from the Court on them and duly served on 5.8.32. Therefore, the Santals lost the land for a paltry sum of Rs. 175/-.

The intense poverty arising out of economically non-viable holdings and land-alienation associated with increase in taxes and abwabs was playing havoc with the Santals. Yet the tribe in general remained above corrupting criminality. Hunter had observed—

"Among pure Santals crime and criminal officers are almost unknown. For some years the Santal district adjoining Beerbhoom was administered on what was termed the 'No-Police system'. The Commissioner (Mr. G.W.Yule) speaks highly of it in his civil and criminal report to government for 1858 (pp. 4,5 & 8) and the Assistant Commissioners who had to carry out its practical details were of one opinion with regard to its success."

On the persual of the contemporary records, there is nothing to indicate that the tribals had taken to crime against property. Rather, Santals enjoy a high reputation for honesty and straight-dealings so much so that the District Gazetteer writes in derision-in connection with the Satyam Shibam Sect, that the Santals were more honest than their so-called civilised brethren. However, some Santals had joined criminal gangs out of extreme poverty.

In Malda District, there were 16 gangs of dacoits in 1930. In only one of them, there were a few Santals. This gang was known as Lalu Halwais Gang-a mixed gang of Santals, Muhammadans and Hindus consisting of 79 members, under the leadership of Lalu Halder of Kalazuri in Gazole police station. There was an outbreak of dacoities and burglaries in Gazole Police station, Malda Police Station and Bangshihari Police Station in Dinajpur district in 1927 and 1928 for which this gang was responsible. Earlier in 1923, a few dacoities had taken place in which the dacoits had shouted Gandhiji-ki-Jai,

Kalimai-Ki-Jai, etc. During the commission of the dacoities, the dacoits did not use unnecessary violence.

Dinajpur district had a concentration of Santal population. There out of 29 dacoit gangs operating in the district two gangs had Santal criminals. Bakshi Kashya's Gang comprised of Santals, Koches and Muslims numbering in all 31, under the leadership of Bakshi Kashya of Panikata in Fulbari PS Another gang consisted of Polias, Santals and Muhammadans numbering 40 under the leadership of Tuna Santal of Dakia in Balurghat Police Station.

Rajshahi district had 10 gangs of dacoits; none was having any Santal.

From a persual of old criminal records, it was found that in some cases, Santals were convicted of petty larceny, like for stealing a goat or five seers of paddy, or like. The cases were rather technical in nature and in most cases, arose out of disputes over ownership of the articles allegedly stolen. It was also seen that most of the complainants happened to be aliens (non-Santals), and we may conjecture the role of the defenceless poor Santals. Apparently, such cases were aimed at dislodging the recalcitrant tribals from the land.

The severity in dealing with the Santals may be observed in the following case:-

Lapso Santal (born in 1899) and Munshi Santal (born in 1883) were two of the persons arrested in connection with Habibpur P.S. Case No. 7 dated 4.9.29 under Section 144/380 IPC. The prosecution story was that these Santals assembled with deadly weapons at the house of Magdo Santal of Rangamatia and looted away maize. The price of the property stolen was Rs. 5/- only. No physical injury was caused to anybody. Yet, in that case, Lapso Santal, Baiznath Santal (Born 1881) and Smt. Champa Majhan, w/o. Jadu Santal were convicted to undergo three months' rigorous imprisonment. Munshi Santal was released on probation of good conduct under Section 562 Cr.P.C. by the Learned Sub-Divisional Officer, Shri M.M. Ghosh on 11.2.29.

As it is, peasants tend to put up, and often positively approve of, a wide variety of crimes induced by poverty. But the collective looting of standing crops from the fields formed a distinct genre of events that disseminated the expressions of insurgency in the rural areas. To the tribals, such activities did not call for any moral approbation or objection, as they heightened the state of the feud between the tribals and the feudal authorities. Such acts were expressions of collective resistance to what the oppressors had been trying to achieve, and signified collective expression of defiance of the lawful authority devoid of the moral fervour. Looting of paddy from alienated land was a protest against the authority dispensing land to others and the morality of such deprivation to the tribals was called in question. While crime in general was considered degrading, collective looting of paddy or fish was deemed a heroic act, a measure of just retribution meted out to the class enemy.

There were two Christian Missions working among the Santals in Barind. One was Protestant Mission, and the other a Catholic one. Father Cattaneo of the Rohanpur Christian Mission (an Italian for that matter) had succeeded Father Anselmo, and had been a nominated member of the District Board, as mentioned earlier. There were about 4000 Christian Santals in Barind. The remaining part of 72000 odds Santal population was divided in halves between the Adi Santals and the Hindu Santals. The Missionaries had all along been helping the converts in mundane matters. They accorded protection to those converts from the machinations of the moeny-lenders and landlords' agents, to their ability and also took up cases to the district administration if needed. Education and health matters of the converts received their keen attention. Conversion was rather a slow process, and in the third decade of the twentieth century, the Christian Missionaries met with a formidable contender in the Hindus who appeared on the scene to convert the tribals into Hinduism. The hope of mundane prosperity had not materialised in regard to the Christian converts, and a spell of conversion to Hinduism followed. Nevertheless, the Missionaries stood by their protege unwaveringly.

At times, this zeal was not appreciated by the administration. The Missionaries had often helped the district administration in appreciating the Santal problem, and had worked on many occasions as the link between the administration and the tribals.

Religion has been a dominating force in the Santal social life. It may be recalled that religion had played an eminent part in the reorganisation of the society on the brink of disintegration. As the sentiments of the society found expression in its songs, so religion became a rallying point to start with. Only through religion, the society could effect a platform wide enough to transcent the barriers of geographical village-federations, to involve the tribal society as a whole. The defensive society sought to create a more satisfying sub-culture, without alienating the principal culture in the proximity. From that point of view, to be Hindus was to initiate process.

It was a brooding tribe that inferred from the defeat of 1855-56 that the tribal gods had failed. The pensive Santals were beset with misfortune after the insurrection of 1855-56 had failed, retributions following quickly. The drought and famine in the following years were playing havoc with them. The dispersal of the tribe to distant places had started, when in 1871, one Bhagirath Manjhi of Godda Subdivision announced that he would restore the Golden Age to the Santals if they returned to the worship of one God and cleaned themselves of their sins. As the king of the new 'Santal Raj' he would show them the way to liberate the country from the oppressors. By advising people to worship the Hindu deity Ram- he identified Ram with the Santal 'Cando'- he assured them that their lands would be recovered. The oppression and maladies that the tribe was passing through were said to be the manifestations of the divine punishment for abandoning the worship of one God and turning to the veneration of minor deities and evil spirits. His teaching was in keeping with the old traditions of the Santals that their ancestors had no Bongas but only worshipped Thakur, the Supreme Deity. As the alienated land could not be recovered, so the followers of 'Bhagrit Baba' started dwindling in number. The Babaji changed his tone of preaching, particularly after the severe famine of 1874, and said that the rebellion had failed on account of sin committed by some of the tribals in having sexual relation with non-Santal women. God or Ram Chando would restore their land only if they purified themselves. He instructed people to take bath before cooking their food, and not to pollute the Burma rice with meat of fowls or pigs.

The preaching of Bhagrit Baba introduced a new element in the Santal psyche, a sense of sin, on terms non-Santal in nature, and prescribed a mode of purification along Hindu lines. It is evident that the Babaji initiated a movement for his race along well defined course, whereas the insurrection of 1855-56 had no such philosophy behind it. The prospect of the 'golden period' or the Santal Raj preached by Babaji was enleavening a hope and he suggested an idealistic path. Later in this book, we shall find that Jitu had also declared independence and established a 'Santal Raj', an object closest to the heart of the Santals- with prospect of introducing analogous system to that prevailing in the 'golden period' of the Santal tradition. The 'Santal Raj' of Bhagrit Baba was a nebulous one, whereas the Santal Raj of Jitu was a reality, though ephemeral. The Kharwar movement initiated by Bhagrit Baba conjured up the Golden Era of the Santal traditions in the minds of the tribals when they lived in Champa in absolute independence and had no rent or tribute to pay but only to bring a small annual offering to their leaders in virtue of their office. That was precisely the call given by Jitu to all Santals in Barind at the time of declaring independence.

The new norms of behaviour which Bhagirath sought to impose on the Santals certainly reflected Hindu notions of purity and pollution. The people, however, were losing faith in him very fast. It was at its ebb when they had to pay for the Burma rice which they had reckoned to be a gift from the government. Bhagrit Baba later tried to make an issue by instigating the Santals not to pay taxes for the land they were cultivating. For this, he was arrested and imprisoned.

After Bhagrit Baba, the movement was kept alive by several preachers who undertook the work on supposed mandates from Ram Cando. The preachings were more religious than political. In 1880 Dubia Gossain introduced the worship of the Babaji in the manner of the Hindus. Gossain himself lived like a Hindu Sannyasi. In 1881, during Census Operations, Gossain instigated the Santals to clamour for a tribal administration. On his advice, as report goes, the Santals objected to the numbering of their houses and the recording of their names. The British government took immediate action; Gossain was arrested and the entire area was placed under police and army.

During the following decades, the Kharwar movement split in three sects-the Sapha Hor, Samra and Babajiu. Safa Hor refers to the sect believing in cleansing one out of impurities from objectionable practices. Samra was the village in Godda Sub division where the founder of this sect lived. Babajiu sprang up from the original group. In practice, however, there was hardly anything to differentiate one group from the other. All the groups worshipped Ram Cando. Later cleavage widened and Sapha Hor with its strict commensal norms turned out to be the more Sanskirtised group. They abandoned what they considered to be degrading practices such as the keeping and eating of fowls and pigs and drinking of 'Handia' or other intoxicants. They could have their morning meal only after taking a purificatory bath. They also recognised Mahadeb as their one God.

The various Bhagat movements had sympathetic vibrations among the Santals. These movements that emerged among the Oraons, Bhils and several other tribes of Chhotanagpur were highly Sanskritised. The closing years of the 19th century saw the advent of a religious leader in Birsa Munda whose preachings were an admixture of Hinduism and Christianity. But the Santals of Barind had no occasion to experience those events as they had already migrated from the Santal Parganas and had all the contacts snapped barring the occasional visits of the preacher of the Babajiu sect. As a result of the Kharwar movement, the Santals were generally moving towards Hinduism. The emulation of Hindu socio-religious practices was regarded as a means of improving their socio-economic status. The preachings of Bongam Majhi and the Janeodhari Santals (Santals wearing sacred threads) may be regarded as the extreme illustration of this school. But in the 1920's political events external to Santal society, helped to check this drift which seemed to be threatening the tribal solidarity. With the spread of the National Freedom Movement, a new political consciousness emerged that engulfed the tribal society. Barind was no exception. "Ideologically, the notion of community is surprisingly resilient. What often happens under the pressure of differentiation and the influence of political ideas and forms of organization brought from outside is a fragmentation of the original idea of the community, an imposition of older cultural symbols of communal identity on a truncated collectivity, such as, for instance, a caste, or a group of artisans, or even a specific stratum of the peasantry. Processes of organised mobilization would then aggregate these turncated communal units into larger political movements".[1]

A continuous first-hand contact between the Santals and the Hindus did create a condition favourable for acculturation and generally led to reciprocal borrowing. The acculturation was intensified with the Kharwar movement and the material conditions prevailing among Santals facilitated it.

Even in the second decade of the 19th century Garos were converted into a form of Hinduism (Baul) by Hindu preachers. Since the 1920's, efforts were made by more than one Hindu organisations to convert the Santals into Hinduism by purificatory rites or 'Suddhi'. The same process was observed in case of the Oraons. The Arya Samaj took the lead in both the cases, but the impact was not felt that keenly there. The Hindu Mission had tried its hand as well, with limited success in Santal Parganas. In fact, the Kharwar movement had

1. Chatterjee, Partha: 'Agrarian Relations and Communalism, 1926-35' in Subaltern Studies, pp. 38

resulted in the adoption of some Hindu rites, beliefs and practices; a few Hindu deities were taken in for worship and Pata and Chhata were added to the cycle of festivals. Already the impact of the Kharwar movement was on the wane and the Arya Samaj and other Hindu Missionaries failed to impress upon the tribals with their abstract conception of God which did not satisfy the emotional needs of the tribals. Another reason why the Arya Samaj failed to impress is that, among Hindus in the surrounding, to be a Hindu was not enough to be tribal. The Arya Samaj did not ascribe any hierarchical placement in the Hindu society and consequently could not convey the lustre of prestige.

'In the Barind, however, the moribund influence of the Kharwar movement pushed the tribe towards Hinduism in a decided way. The Satyam Shibam sect was almost a continuation of the Kharwar movement without a break, with the additional prospect of better placement of the converts in the Hindu caste hierarchy. A new polity and leadership developed in Barind, as against the traditional leadership, projecting a new ideal for acceptance of the society, in order to achieve a goal. The caste and creed differences were melting away in the face of a new upsurge of national objective-freedom from the foreign yoke. To be a party to this new wave, it was necessary to come out of the shell of isolation and join the mainstream. The Santals responded to the call of the Swarajists in 1921, and to identify themselves totally, they obliterated the difference in religion to a great extent. It will be seen that the converts to Hinduism had taken the lead in the movements in Barind. It is also to be noted that the Santals in Barind were launching movements against the landlords primarily to resist enhancements of rent since 1907. The dominant society in the environment was Hindu. The conversion might have been motivated by an inaccurate expectation that by conversion, the tribals would come closer to the Hindus,. thereby, broadening the prospect of cooperation and sympathy from the Hindus. Besides, conversion holds a prospect of mundane prosperity. The movements of the Santals in Barind were to wrest economic freedom from the strangle-hold of the Hindu neighbours. All these factors together made the Santals accept Hinduism as a religion.

Religion is an integral part of the Santal's existence. The inspiration to do difficult jobs on the mundane plane springs from the mandate of Gods. It may be recalled that Sido-Kanhu had mandates from God to launch the movement which rolled into a rebellion of great force. In case of Jitu at Barind, he also talked to Goddess Kali in his dream. He was also in possession of an amulet believed to accord supernatural protection to him. Even the charisma attributed to Jitu was a projection of the tribal belief in the supernatural.

Bharat Sevasram Sangha was started at Bajitpur in Faridpur district (now in Bangladesh) by Swami Pranabanandaji in 1917, with Hindu ideals of Brahmacharya and patriotic ideas. While Pranabanandaji was the President, Swami Satyananda alias Kalyan Kumar Nag was the General Secretary. They were the guiding spirits of the movement. But a difference in opinion led to a rift between the two and Swami Satyananda parted company in May 1926. With about 150 members and headquarters at 65/1, College Street, he started the Hindu Mission, and started a train of conversions. Swami Satyananda was closely linked with the Hindu Sabha and the Suddhi movement of which the late Ghanashyamdas Birla was a patron. The other notable person in the Hindu Sabha was Shri Padmaraj Jain. Later, Hindu Mission and Hindu Sabha worked hand in hand in propagating the Hindu ideals and in arranging the conversion of ethnic groups of people standing in the periphery of the Hindu society at large. The extension of the Muslim preponderance and steep rise in population had been unnerving to the discerning Hindu social leaders. The conversion was a reaction to that fear of imbalance.

This movement was not unique in Bengal. Even as the non-cooperation and the Khilafat movements were in progress, a section of Muslim leaders saw it fit to urge the Muslims to form associations that would give an expression of the Muslim mind in India. The Khilafat Committees were not considered enough for the purpose as, in their reckoning, those committees were greatly influenced by Congress. This section of the Muslim leaders appreciated Congress as a Hindu organ. In May 1922, Maniruz-Zaman Islamabadi toured the mufassil areas of Bengal advocating formation of Jamiat-ul-Ulema. His plan (it is said that the plan had actually emanated from Maulana Azad Sobhani) was to form a Jamiat in each district, each of which again will elect an Amir-i-Balad. From amongst those Amirs a Sheikh-ul-Islam would be elected for the whole of India. The object of the scheme was to secure the full expression of Muslim opinion and protect Muslim interests, for which purpose the Khilafat Committees, controlled as they often were by Hindus, were not considered satisfactory.

In a state of mutual suspicion and apathy, the Hindus were organising themselves. In December 1922, a Kshatriya conference was held in Calcutta at 4, Sovaram Basak Street which was presided over by Gopal Singh of Khandwar (near Ajmer). Prominent political workers like Bholanath Barman, Madhu Prasad Sukul and Ambica Prasad Bajpai attended the conference.

The conversion of Malkana Muhammadans to Hinduism by Swami Sraddhanand in March 1923 in Rajputana created excitement amongst Muslim leaders so much so that the attention of the Muslims in India was diverted to that direction from the Khilafat movement. The reaction was strong and the Muslim leaders associated with the Khilafat movement sent out appeals to the Muslims not to precipitate trouble on that account. The Anzuman-Waizine Hanifia Bangala, of which Moulana Abu Bakr was the President, took the lead in whipping up Muslim sentiment.

Swami Sraddhanand was an Arya Samaji, but the Moulana's supporters were somehow convinced that the Swami was working under instructions from Congress leaders Madan Mohan Malaviya and Motilal Nehru. In April 1923, seven meetings were held in Calcutta to concert measures to counteract the action of Swami Sraddhanand. While subscriptions were being requested by Hindus for 'Suddhi' ceremony, Muslims projected a counter-threat of converting Hindus into Islam. Apart from conversion, branches of Hindu Sabha were set up in the districts with definite programme of propaganda and conversion. Wandering preachers were also sent to various places to make the Hindus alive to the threat looming large on the horizon. There was a branch at Malda of which Shri Ashutosh Chowdhury one of the richest landlords of Malda was a patron. In other districts also rich Zamindars were patronising the Hindu Sabha. In Malda, Ashutosh Choudhury wrote a letter to Padmaraj Jain on 23.3.28 in the capacity of Secretary, regarding delegates to be sent to Mymensing. Six delegates were sent from Malda and they were Ashutosh Chowdhury, Madan Mohan Satiar (Merchant), Narayan Chandra Saha (Merchant), Krishna Gopal Sen Kaviraj, Kailash Nath Roy and Bholanath Chowdhury.

The Hindu revivalistic movement had resorted to conversion as a method of increasing the Hindu ranks. It has been urging the Hindu society to take note of the dismal picture around, of the countless events of torture on Hindus, and urging them to be united to repulse the attack on the Hindu way of life. A state of great excitement was built up, by lectures, lantern-shows and blown-up accounts of heroic deeds against molestations. Great landlords and Zamindars were taking interest in the movements. The Maharaja of Dinajpur was willing to be a patron of the Hindu Sabha opened at Dinajpur. Though the association of Kashiswar Chakraborty of Dinajpur with the Hindu Sabha could not be definitely established, his activities in Barind among the Santals had taken definite shape. He was highly revered by the Santals as the Great Preceptor (Thakur Baba). Shri Chintaharan Mukherjee, another lawyer of Dinajpur was the Secretary of the Dinajpur branch of Hindu Sabha for some time; then the assignment was taken over by Shri Bijoy Ranjan Mitra. The Hindu Sabha at Malda was opened much later and there is nothing to indicate that the Hindu Sabha paid much attention to Barind and the Santals there. It was during this period that a spell of conversion to Hinduism started inducting ethnic groups as Kshatriyas. It would appear that the induction spear-headed through the Hindu Mission was limited to those ethnic groups which had been able to establish themselves as permanent agricultural village communities. The Rajbanshies and the Hajangs became Kshatriyas around that time. Corresponding social intention was discernible among these ethinc groups in movements launched by them severally. Records of the Rajbanshi Kshatriya Samity, Fulbari Centre, Jagannathpur, in Dinajpur district indicated that 1262 Bratya Kshatriyas (popularly known as Rajbanshies) took up the sacred thread on the 24th, the 25th and the 26th July, 1928. Pandit Digendra Narayan Bhattacharya, Bidyabhusan of Sirajganj (Pabna: presently in Bangladesh) and others had taken up the work of the priests in the ceremony. These people had assembled from the neighbouring six villages. The conversion of Rajbanshies at Hili (Bogra: now in Bangladesh) with much fanfare may also be mentioned here. Letters from Swami Satyananda indicated that about five thousand such persons became Hindus at Hili alone. There (at Hili) Maharaja Sashi Kanta Acharya Chaudhuri of Mymensing read a printed address advocating the necessity of Suddhi and reformation of the Hindu society. In the conference, Moulana Akram Khan's brother, a new convert, was presented with an introduction by Shri Narendra Narayan Chakraborty of Pabna. Dr. Sunity Kumar Chatterjee presided over the Hindu Yubak Sammilanee on the 6th March 1928. For the purpose of extending the activities of the Hindu Mission help was requested from the Hindu Sabha which was having great many wealthy patrons all over the country. It is significant that the Hindu Mission did not attempt to convert the Santals of Barind to Hinduism though it had started working among the Santals in the Santal Parganas within its means. It may be recalled that in 1930, Bongam Manjhi started a movement in the Santal Parganas wherein the Santals were taking sacred threads; they were known as 'Janeo-dharis'. These Santals (janeodharies) considered themselves socially superior to others and were very puritan (in the Hindu recknoning) in attitude. This sect had taken up the exclusive use of khadi clothing and urged people not to dance anywhere except in their own villages. They had all other observances of the Sapha Hor. Had Hindu Mission assured the Santals of Kshatriya status, like the Rajbanshies and Hajangs, perhaps the movement of Bongam Manjhi would never have arisen. As such, it may be presumed that the assurance of higher placement in the Hindu social hierarchy as reportedly given to the Santals in Barind was not from the Hindu Mission or Hindu Sabha. As Kashiswar Chakraborty was the mentor of the tribals in Barind, he might have given an assurance to that effect; but we do not find any mention of such an assurance given by the preacher anywhere other than the chronicle. As an individual, he was perhaps not in a position to effect such an upliftment in status of the Santals. Besides, ascribing such status is dependent on acceptance by others in the Hindu society. From a letter written to Padmaraj Jain, of Hindu Relief Committee (a committee of the Hindu Sabha), it appears that Kashiswar Chakraborty was keen to be a member of the Hindu Sabha. This letter was written by Kashiswar Chakraborty on 26.11.26. It may be mentioned in passing that by that time, substantial number of Santals in Barind, including Jitu and Arjun, had already been converted to Hinduism and the movements in the Barind were progressing towards its culmination. May be Kashiswar Chakraborty had a mind to join the Hindu Sabha, a body, which might have conferred higher social status on to the Santal converts. The conferment of higher social status by a body would have better chances of acceptance to the society in general, rather than such act of a lone preacher. Even ethnic groups accorded Kshatriya status were not accepted as such by the other Hindus. This may be one of the reasons why such movements died down after a short while.

Various associations were sprouting up in the district in response to calls given by national leaders, primarily to discuss the nationalist ideas, problems and for exchange of ideas. In Malda, the Maithili a dominant Brahman society living in Englishbazar and Kaliachak thanas, formed an association styled All India Maithil Youngmen Society, Malda. The first anniversary of the society was observed on the 10th Novermber 1929 at Araidanga, Malda. Pandit Khealiram Jha, Vice-President of Mathura-Agra Maithil Mahasammilan, presided over the anniversary functions. This anniversary was presented as the Akhil Bhartiya Maithil Yubak Sammilan, i.e. All India Maithil Youth Conference wherein Kumar Gangan-and Sinha, MLA of Srinagar, district Purnea, Bihar was the President. About 400 delegates attended the conference, of whom forty came from other districts and provinces. Shri Pramatha Nath Misra, a pleader of the local Bar was the president of the Reception Committee. Pandit Newalal Mishra of Bhagalpur was also present in the conference. Atul Chandra Kumar of Araidanga and Bhpuendranath Jha of Nagharia had also taken part in the deliberations.

The All Bengal Provincial Hindu Conference was held at Malda on the 17th and the 18th September 1932 under the Presidentship of Ramananda Chattarji, Editor, the Probasi and the Modern Review. More than a thousand assembled under a pandal erected for the purpose. The gathering included some ladies and members from the depressed classes and Santals. Notable persons present in the meeting were Jyotirmohan Misra as Chairman of the Reception Committee, Shrimati Sarla devi Choudhurani, Padmaraj Jain and Prof. Binay Sarkar. A resolution was passed requesting Swami Satyananda, Shri Haridas Majumdar and Shri Jogeswar Mandal who had already left for Bombay by then, to attend the conference convened by Pandit Madan Mohan Malaviya and to strive in collaboration with Dr. Moonje for settlement of the problem concerning the depressed classes on the lines adopted at the conference as far as practicable.

The flurry among the Hindus had its impact on the Muslims. On 27th October 1929, a meeting was organised by all the Muhammadans of Araidanga and Chandpur villages in Ratua thana, at the house of a dismissed Sub-Inspector of Police named Mubarak Ali Khan of Araidanga, in which a Muhammadan association styled 'Malda Moslem Yubak Sangha' was formed. The office-bearers were influenced by Atul Chandra Kumar. The aims and objectives of this association were reportedly to raise social, political and economic status of the Muslims of the district. The word 'yubak' nevertheless, it was clearly stated that Muhammadans of all ages having enthusiasm of youth might be enlisted as members. Munshi Yakub Ali, a teacher of Araidanga High English School was the President of the association. Kazi Reasat Hossain and Mubarak Ali Khan of Araidanga were made the Vice-Presidents, whereas Ahmed Ali Khan of Araidanga was made the Secretary. Mubarak Ali had been known for his participation in the non-cooperation movement. Wahed Bux (the Treasurer and Assistant Secretary) was a close friend of Atul Chandra Kumar.

It may be mentioned in passing that the saner elements of both the communities-Hindu and Muslim-were working together in the cause of the nationalist movement. There were, however, other sections in both the communities susceptible to communal ideas arising out of a host of reasons following inadequate economic development in the country, creating disparities and sparse opening for middle class educated gentry. Aspirations led to scramble and communal identity was thrust as a point in the bargain. The political parties feared loss of support from the petty bourgeois and kept silent over communal issues, or compromised with communal overtures.

The waves of non-cooperation movement had reached the district of Malda. A new awareness of duties and responsibilities to the nation had been permeating the society. The youth also reacted. Gymnasiums and libraries were coming up gradually, and those afforded the youth to gather and get enlightenment. The Youth Association was the principal political organisation, established in 1927 as a response to the call of Netaji Subhas Chandra Bose. A local youth of indomitable spirit, Atul Chandra Kumar, and his associates Jyotirmoy Sharma, Sudhir Kumar Raha and others formed this association with the motto of 'unity'. It was believed that their object was to spread communism, a fact not borne by subsequent developments. What Atul Kumar and his friends could achieve was to convey a sense of awakening to reality and unrest in the middleclass society. They made use of the Saraswati Library started by Shri Dwarka Prasad Behani, son of Sarjoo Prasad Behani a rich merchant of the town. Sarjoo Behani was

President and financer to the district Congress. This library had a good collection of published work considered objectionable by the government at that time. The boys had been using the gymnasium at the Hindu Dharmashala and at Mokdampur in the town. Malda Youth Association was affiliated to All Bengal Youth Association at Calcutta.

Forming of association was followed up by publishing periodical for the dissemination of ideas among the reading public. Saraswati Library was receiving attention of the local administration as the rendezvous of the fiery youth of the locality. The 'Mahananda', an organ of the association was brought out. Lal Behari Majumdar Kaviraj, the then Assistant Secretary of the district Congress was made the editor, though Sudhir Kumar Raha, a fiery youth of the town was the de facto editor. Bengali publication Mahananda was started in September 1927. Four youngmen of Malda town-Sarbashri Balaram Halder, Sudhir Kumar Raha, Nirmalapada Chatarji, Fani Bhusan Sarkar-took the initiative. The magazine was intended to be published bi-monthly from Bipin Memorial Pathagar. When its second issue came out six more persons joined the team of management. They were Jyotirmoy Sharma, Sailendranath Majumdar, Jyotindra Nath Sinha (a teacher of Nagharia H.E.School), Jagabandhu Roy of Kaligram, Bidhubhusan Jha of Nagharia and Nishanath Sarkar of Kaligram. The contributors were the youths of Malda. The magazine was published from Gourdut press. Sudhir Kumar Raha and Sailaja Kumar Bhattacharjee were the assistant editors. The first two issues caused a flutter in the administrative circle and the editor dissociated himself from the magazine as the tone of the publication was not to his liking. From the third issue, the management of the magazine was transferred to the Tarun Sahitya Sammilanee from the Bipin Memorial Pathagar; Sudhir Kumar Raha took up as the editor. After its fourth issue published in the middle of 1928, under the management of the members of the Tarun Sahitya Sammilanee of Malda, the Mahananda ceased to breathe. The ostensible reasons were lack of funds and public apathy. Sudhir Kumar Raha had to leave his uncle's house at Malda where he was staying and Shri Atul Chandra Kumar was drawn away to Calcutta.

Thus it would seem that though the youth of the town and the prosperous areas of the district in the Tal and the Diara regions was seething, eager to take part in the freedom struggle against the British rule and responding to the directions of the leaders like Netaji Subhas Chandra Bose and the Mahatma, yet no firm link between them and the Santals of Barind had been established to forge a unity in the struggles for the common cause. Notably, these youths came from middle-class families and had their own familial backgrounds in reckoning the movement and participating in that. On the other hand, the Santals had the question of survival at the back of their minds, and land happened to be behind all moves. To them, freedom meant abolition of rent for the land they were cultivating; freedom meant liquidation of the vexatious abwabs and exactions. To them, freedom meant a journey to the Golden Era of their traditions, without hindrance from the landlords and their agents and the money-lenders. The rhetorical references to a state of freedom conjured up these elements in the minds of the tribals, and in the meetings held in the town, they had heard of social regeneration, and development and welfare of the depressed classes. It may be recalled that in the meeting of the All Bengal Provincial Hindu Conference at Malda on the 17th and the 18th September 1932, the gathering included some members of the depressed classes and Santals.

The presence of Santals was noticed in another meeting at Malda. The Youth Conference was held on the 7th and the 8th November 1928 at which Mr. Philip Spratt, Shri Dharani Kanta Goswami and Dr. Bhupendranath Dutta addressed the gathering. The meetings were not largely attended, but the sessions on the first day were graced by the presence of ladies. The speakers confined themselves to an exposition of the principles of communism and what it would do for the peasants and workers. Shri Dharani Kanta Goswami explained in details in Bengali the speech of Mr. Philip Spratt, and observed that 'I notice today a unique feature in your meeting. I find before me a gathering of some people of the depressed classes. It appears to me that the youngmen's society of Malda has directed attention towards people belonging to the lower stratum of society-people whom we are used to hate as of low origin. I have not come across people of such a class in any other youth association or any national institution. I am not sure if you have seen any.'

The presence of odd Santals in the meetings called by the youth or the elites of the Hindu society at Malda did not actually reveal the extent of mixing of the tribals with the Hindus to merge themselves with the mainstream of the freedom movement. Nor did it reveal the quantum of Hindu influence on the tribals. It is better to recall that the Hindus were the dominant aggressive society in the environ, and the Santals had been suffering actually on account of land-alienation due to the Hindus mostly. The land was being grabbed by the money-lenders, non-agriculturists and the landlords and their men. At time, even after alienation, a part of the land was allowed to the Santal to till, and after harvest, considerable portions of produce were going out of Barind. There could not have been an amity between the Hindus and the Santals unless the discrimination and inequity were brought down to a bearable degree. The defensive social stance of the tribe sought to reduce the alienation of the dominant society by way of accepting the same religion. That is why the Santals in large number embraced Hinduism, and found out a common enemy. The political awareness of the day did not sink deep in the psyche of the tribals. The political ideals of the day were beyond the comprehension of the average tribal. But they had reckoned the politics of resistance to the administration, and devised their own method. Since the tribe was having an agricultural bias-though they had failed by then to establish themselves as a permanent agricultural community-they planned out their resistance by withholding payment of taxes to the landlords. They were allergic to abwabs generally and gave the call to stop payment of any such abwabs; rather a conscious attempt was made to revive the days of the golden era. The movements-national or local, did not influence the course of the tribal movement to a great extent. The tribals drew upon their traditions and was bent on creating a Raj for themselves when the yoke of the foreign rule was shaken off. It was the concept of the community as a collective whole that created the personality in Jitu who took up leadership in the locality. To them, Gandhiji was a name to conjure with and they had invoked the name of Gandhi Raj ascribing suzerain power to him. To them, the days of the British Raj were at an end, and Gandhi Raj would dawn on any of the days. From that point of view, it would be fair to infer that the Santals of Barind drew their inspiration from the Great Leader in Gandhiji, as was done by their more civilised brethren the Hindus. It may be recalled that the peasants of Awadh had evinced similar belief while pushing ahead their movement in 1920-21. Among the Santals, the great wave of the national movement created a deep impression. Yet they perceived the programme in the light of their comprehension. In the semi-conscious mental recesses, the image of the Great Leader Gandhi was too high and the adoration for him matched the spirit of the tribal sense or greatness; emulation came automatically. It was the Raj-British Raj replaced by the Gandhi Raj-that had fascinated the tribals. They mixed up the streams of movement and conceived their own ideas and programmes. Movement went in the name of Gandhi. He was the overlord, while Jitu would be the king and in the kingdom, a basketful of paddy would be the tax due to the king.

Another streak of movement-largely comprising of Hindu youths-had however, been moving in Barind. The intensity of anarchist movement was increasing in the district and the then Superintendent of Police, Mr. H.B. Miller, had advised the government of a reported plan by the anarchists to utilise the Adina Mosque or the ruins of Gaur as repository of their arms and weapons. It appeared that the anarchists had intensified their activities in the district throughout 1933. Not less than 130 members belonging to various terrorist groups (Jugantar, Anushilan and Communist groups) could be located by the law enforcing agency.

The intense economic plight had been a cause of the upsurge. The traditions held a hope of restoring a society free from the economic bondage. The intense desire to have absolute mastery over land so that a permanent agricultural society could be established without alien interference, coupled with a spirit of independence happened to be the driving force behind the Santal upsurges. The aim was to set up principalities under tribal leadership. This sentiment was not the outcome of a political consciousness, but the idea of revivalism tinged with past glory of the tribe and a projection of the socio-cultural continum. The golden days of Champa was a lure to the tribal mind. The variations in the processes were due to an awareness of the local conditions.

It is also apparent that new leadership developed during the process of resurgence, to which the traditional leadership succumbed. Even during the days of Jitu, there was a Parganait living within Habibpur thana. His authority was quietly brushed aside. The charisma or grace of God was a necessity to transcend the limit of societal leadership. That is why Sido Kanhu were established as charismatic leaders or 'Subha Thakur' by smearing vermillion and oil on them. The temporal and the spiritual leadership had to be merged in one. Yet, the method that the new leadership had adopted during the struggle was age-old. The leaders had created and continued a spell of excitement and tension within the tribe. The compulsions of the society and believers forced the leader to undertake projects to satisfy the urge of the followers, irrespective of the danger in such projects. The sequence of events at Adina Mosque would be a sure indication to that.

To the Santals, Barind was a conclave. They had crossed the Ganges at Rajmahal and that remained as the dividing line with their cultural motherland-the Santal Parganas. The group of people settling down at Barind had all connections snapped, except odd one or two preceptors of the Sapha Hor sect coming to the Barind to communicate, may be once a year. In the alien surroundings, they did not find much except hard labour to clear the jungles, to break the virgin land and eke out an existence. They had proceeded along tribal lines, creating villages on either side of the road (Kulahi) and recreating tribal culture. The Santal institutions were set up as far as they could ensure. But the social leadership had been weakening since long. This phenomenon was observed by O'Malley in Bankura around 1910 even. Here at Barind, the social leadership developed limping, without any power to hold land for the community. It may also be mentioned that there was no Santal inhabitant earlier in Malda district, like Midnapore, Birbhum, Bankura, Purulia or Burdwan. But the mirgants had the rueful experience of exploitation at the hands of the so-called civilised people, like they had experienced in the Santal Parganas; hence at Barind they were wary. In Barind, the exploitation did not go to the extent of bondage though. The Santals in Barind found themselves in the proximity of other depressed classes like Turi, Jalua Kaibartas, Polis and Rajbanshies, who were having identical problems of living. The group-solidarity of the Santal had led them to the fore.

The tradition of the Santals is replete with stories of kings and queens and princes-a clean indication of the line of thinking of the tribals. In fact, these stories are uncomplicated ones wherein the royal personage is an extension of the social leadership. We have already mentioned king Jaura. The idea of kingship had been an alien thought to the Santals. The golden era of Santal traditions even do not project any picture on that score. Interestingly, the instances of kingship referred to in Santal traditions are preceded by migration or conversion of the tribal elite aristocracy to Hinduism. We may mention Panchayat or Saont. The idea of kingship has been irretrievably linked with power and freedom from interference from aliens. The tribe had migrated to Barind, the new elite group had been formed, conversion to Hinduism was accomplished, and we shall see how the charismatic leader established the Santal Raj.

Some part of Malda is always in distress. The rainfall is scanty, and in Barind, the retentive capacity of the soil is much less than other places. The rainfall is generally unevenly distributed. The average rainfall has been noted to be around 52 inches a year. Barind is particularly vulnerable to drought, and the Western part of the district suffers from the ravages of drought and flood.

In 1930, there was distress in the south of the district, mainly in Shibgunj thana. It may be recalled that 1930 was a year of normal rainfall (Census : 1951). The distress was caused by floods, and extensive agricultural loans had to be distributed. The paddy in Nachole thana and part of Nawab-ganj thana was attacked by a root disease which spoiled the crop. There were generally poor crops all over the district, especially the Rabi crop which gave a poor yield to a complete drought from the middle of February 1931 to the end of May 1931. This also delayed the sowing of Aus paddy, jute and Amon seedlings.

Agricultural loans on a large scale had to be distributed in Shibgunj, Nawabganj and Nachole thanas in May and June 1931, to enable the raiyats to buy seed. The rate was fixed at -/8/- annas per bigha, with a maximum of Rs. 10/- per head. The average loan was worked out to Rs. 7/8/- only. The total amount distributed thus was Rs. 13000/-. The result of timely help was reaped in a splendid crop of Aus-the best within a decade in those areas, barring one or two Unions of Nawab-ganj where the Bhadoi was damaged by flood which caught it owing to the late sowing. But prices ruled low and though starvation could be staved off, the economic condition of cultivators remained the same. The district administration insisted on collecting loans in October, except in affected Unions, out of the proceeds of Bhadoi harvest.

However, further loans had to be given in those thanas in July 1931 for weeding operations. Two reasons were assigned for that: firstly, without loans most of the fields would not have been weeded and an indifferent crop would have resulted; secondly, the landless labourers were at starvation point as nobody had any money to employ them. About Rs. 22000/- was distributed in Shibgunj and Nawabganj thanas in July 1931 for weeding operations at the general flat rate of Rs. 5/-per head.

Although the rest of the thanas had managed to sow their fields without help, it became clear in July that help must be given in the Tal area of Harischandrapur and Kharba thanas where for three years running the crops had been poor. This was the area immediately south of the railway line. Rs. 6000/- was distributed in loans for weeding in this area in the middle of July and the help of the zamindars and the Samshi merchants was enlisted to grant loans in kind on a large scale.

It was touch and go whether Ratua and Kaliachak thanas would pull through without help, but they did.

In the first week of August there was a bad flood of the Mahananda which inundated extensive areas in Kharba, Harischandrapur and Ratua thanas. The Aus paddy was caught in flowers owing to the late sowing and over a large part of Ratua thana was destroyed together with a large crop of maize, an important subsidiary in that thana.

Flood-water drained off from Kharba and Harischandrapur thanas quicker than it did from Ratua and little or no damage was done north of the railway line. Damage in the Tal area was not so severe as in Ratua. Rs. 23000/- was distributed in Ratua, Harischandrapur and Kharba thanas as maintenance loans at the end of August. The District Magistrate toured the area in September and told the people that no more maintenance loans would be given and that, for their maintenance, they must send their menfolk to neighbouring thanas and districts to earn money harvesting the bumper crops. Labour was fetching three annas so that acute distress was not present. The Magistrate assured further loan at the rate of -/8/- annas per bigha for seed early in October. The people accepted this assurance satisfactorily. They wanted to know if Test Relief Works would be started in November, if necessary. The Magistrate assured the people that arrangements has already been made with the District Board and government had by then been approached for a sum of Rs. 5000/- for the Test Relief Works. He hoped that the request would be granted, as in other cases. Close watch on Ratua thana was also kept to ascertain if Test Relief Work would be necessary there.

Maintenance loans had to be given because in the rains no Test Relief Work was possible.

About Rs. 20000/- was distributed as seed loans in Ratua and Kharba thanas at the beginning of October, as well as Rs. 1200/- in gratuitous relief. Rs. 1000/- was distributed as seed loan in Gazole thana in one Union which had suffered from flood. It was not found necessary to distribute any loan in the south of the district as the damage done by the flood there was comparatively slight. It was also thought that remission of the July loan in those Unions in which the crop that had been financed was destroyed by flood, should be considered by the Circle Officer Samshi after the Puja.

Collections of the May and June loans in the south of the district were made in October. There was a lot of requests turned down. The district administration, however, advised the loan collectors to collect from persons who could pay. It was decided that no certificate would be issued and fresh attempts to collect loans would be made after February 1932.

In addition to ordinary agricultural loans, about Rs. 5000/- was distributed in 1931 as sericultural loans to silk-growers in order to enable them to buy coccoons from the government nursery. This industry was very much depressed owing to the low prices ruling in the silk market, and what was once a flourishing and lucarative industry was steadily declining. There was a possibility that the action of Congress in getting some mills to boycott foreign yarn might help revive the silk industry. In response to inquiries, sample of yarns were sent to several mills.

Economic distress in the district was accentuated owing to three factors :- Firstly, the silk market had brought in a lot of hard cash when it was flourishing. Secondly, the failure of the lac industry. The third factor was the failure of three years running of the mango crop. Malda mangoes are famous and they bring in much hard cash into the district. In addition, there were various minor subsidiary industries dependent on the mango crop, most of which support the poorer classes.

And of course, the old custom of allowing the windfalls to anybody who could pick it up was a boon to many. The mangoes are rich in vitamins and the poor classes get a good store of these inside them in years of plenty which help them to withstand disease. It was believed that a bad mango year was always a bad malaria year on account of lack of vitamins. This was certainly true in 1930, and progressively, a very bad malaria epidemic had spread in the district.

In fact, in Barind, crop had been failing since 1928, following the drought of 1927. No relief worth the name was sent there. The elaborate care for the ravaged areas elsewhere in the district was singularly absent in Barind. Apart from a seed loan of Rs. 1000/- distributed in Gazole thana, no assistance worth the name was given to the Santals in Barind. The loans granted to the Santals earlier had piled up and the bumper Amon crop in 1930 encouraged the administration to exact the arrears with fair amount of rigidity. This was discrimination, to say the least, to the Santals who were left to the mercy of God and the predators who had been gobbling up the land of the tribals.

Some of the peasant movements of India during the British rule were characterised by endeavours to establish 'independent' kingdoms free of extraneous exploitation and coercion. The movement of Samsher Gazi in Tripura during the 18th Century (1767-68), the first Garo insurrection in Mymensingh during the 19th Century (1825-27), the Wahabi Movement (1830), the Farazi rebellion (1838-48), the Santal Hul of 1855-56 were some of the instances.

In all the cases, extreme coercion and exploitation led the peasants to insurrection, and behind the insurrections the will to establish kingdoms for themselves, to rid of the rampant exploitation of outsiders or agencies imposed on them, was paramount. It may be recalled that at least three of the above movements started as religious reform movements. Religious reforms helped the Garos to unite and see things in a new perspective. The Santal Hul of 1855-56 was motivated by a will to establish a kingdom for themselves, though the inhuman torture and exploitation had a great role in pushing the Santals ahead. The role of religion in the Santal movements has already been discussed. In all the the struggle was evidently for obtaining the real control over land whereon the heart of the peasant lay[2].

The movement of Santals in Barind had started as a peasant movement initially. The insecurity over land, the rapacious demands of the money-lenders and landlords and their agents, the vagaries of seasonal cultivation in a mono-crop area and periodical droughts had been cutting at the roots of the hope of affluence. Steady alienation of land accentuated the misery of the peasants. And the movement had started in which peasants from other communities joined. In fact, proliferation of the movement was noticed as the waves of non-cooperation movement lashed at Malda. It happened that in the second half of the nineteenth century the state no longer remained the sole appropriator of the agrarian surplus. With the growth of intermediaries and the beginning of capitalist agriculture characterised by absentee landlordism, the ties of paternalism steadily declined in the country side. A corresponding change in the characteristic of the peasant movement was also noticed in that traditional leaders no longer led movements, and the Zamindars replaced the state as the main target of attack.

Peasant communities acting autonomously against the formally organised state, or its agents or functionaries, tend to organise the members of the community on the most convenient issue of projecting the state as an oppressive apparatus. This is possible due to a perceptual distance from the members of such communities to the state which attains an impersonal attitude, and is greatly facilitated in the absence of adequate communication between the two elements. It is not always that differences in respect of other forms of identity are merged in the peasant identity alone. Diverse groups may participate in the peasant movement. The points of difference

2. Ray, Suprakash, Bharater Krishak-Bidroha O Ganatantrik Sangram, p. 204

may affect intra-group relationships which are guided by their considerations simultaneously. The solidarity of the peasant movement in Barind was adversely affected as the Muslims drew themselves away from the movement in 1924. Ostensibly, difference of opinion arose over the mode of utilisation of the collected subscription from the peasants. It may be recalled that by the end of 1923, Congress had withdrawn its support from any militant peasant movement in the country. Added to this, there was much anxiety over the reactions of ardent members of the Satyam Shibam sect who allegedly wanted to establish hegemony of the converted Hindu tribals in the area. That would have hurt the Muslims no doubt. From 1911 onwards, many Muslim settlers had come down to Barind from other places, buying land and cultivating. Any strong movement against land alienation would have the potentiality of dislodging them from their acquired possessions. The split in the Congress over the communal question had also come around this time and the Muslims in Malda in general had responded to the exhortations of Muslim leaders who were keen to organise the Muslims in all the districts. All these factors prompted the Muslims to get away from the peasant movement in Barind. The Rajbanshies and Polis were settled agriculturists, and were not plagued by land alienation in general; they had adjusted themselves with the money economy long back. They were generally swayed by the call of non-cooperation movement and with the withdrawal of the Congress support, and with the gradual increase in violence in the movement, they also delinked themselves from the agitation.

Violence in Barind centred round retention of possessions over land by the Santals as also looting of standing crop from the field. The Santals did not venture to attack the kutcheries of the landlords or the money-lenders to get the loan-papers back, as it happened in many other districts. Violence was resorted to, when necessity arose, to exert traditional rights like fishing rights in the beels and jalkars. And violence was adopted as a means of securing greater degree of solidarity resulting out of an extensive conditioning of the impending struggle. The new Santal leadership was successful to a great extent in drawing out the tribals from the defensive shell, conditioned them to ideals of a desired goal, and led them in the struggle. While the Santals were conscious about their peasant identity, they were conscious about the goal as well as a Raj for themselves. The Santals in Barind did not go for wanton destruction or looting of foodgrains and kept themselves confined to a minimum exercise of violence. This was possible as the leadership could control the masses within reasonable limits. As long as the tribals maintained their contact with the non-cooperation movement, they were having the benefit of an asymmetrical movement initiated by Gandhiji. But when other communities parted company, and the tribe adopted the line of tribal revivalism, they reverted to the process of symmetrical opposition-arms against arms, condign against the condign. The rationale of an asymmetrical process of resistance was beyond the comprehension of the Santal. In the psyche of the Santal, power is irretrievably associated with the condign, an invariable attribute of the king who also controls land as a source of income. To this goal-to attain power by having their own Raj-the Santals have ever been proceeding. Insurgency was no more than a point in the life of the Santal peasants. The stream of consciousness about the final goal- a Raj unto themselves - has ever been flowing underneath and urging them to find new channels to achieve it. Insurgency was means to that end. In Barind, the Santals transcended the sphere of peasant insurgency and sought to curve out their own Raj. To that end, the social will had projected a charismatic leader in Jitu Sardar.

Another significant feature of the Santal insurgency in Barind was that women were kept out of the proceedings mostly. Unlike the Hul, attributing charisma to Jitu did not accompany coercion on women in any way. Rather, women were allowed to perform worship of the Goddess Kali set up by Jitu, and the tribals accepted such role of women without any seeming protest. It will also be seen that a Santal woman was brought to the Adina Mosque to be elevated to the position of the queen - as given out by Jitu's daughter. In another version, the Santal maid was brought to Adina Mosque to be married to Saona, a lieutenant of Jitu. It will be observed that women generally were accorded more consideration, and a Hindu influence is discernible in the matter. In the Santal insurrection of 1855-56, no such consideration was displayed by the leaders. Branding of Santal women as witches for refusing to observe rituals for Hul, and access of Sido-Kanhu to Santal women have been mentioned in the accounts of Chotrae Desmanjhie. The rituals prior to the insurrection were part of conditioning of the tribals to insurgency[3]. Access to the tribal women was an expression of overlordship and the brothers sought to establish their temporal as well as spiritual leadership over the tribe and the rituals were in part the sacramental necessities of such overlordship.

The subordinate position of women in the tribe is a fact, arising out of reorganisation of society into a defensive one, the tribals not recognizing any responsibility to the weakening economic condition and other maladies. Black magical power was attributed to women and a connection to the Bonga was brought into belief. The control over Bongas was exercised by women supposedly through sexual powers and magical incantations. The basic motivating power was envy. Attributing all the motive to envy is an indication of the tribe's urge for possession of mundane attributes. Like any other society, Santal women are also exploited by the dominating male. Myths were created by the male-dominated society to condition the members in the belief, in a bid to weaken the family, to perpetuate domination of the society over the individual and the family. During the movement in Barind, Santal women were not subjected to any such tyranny and excess. Nor were the Santal women of Barind required to travel with their husbands from place to place, gathering whatever they found in route. By and large, the Santals in Barind were not required to leave their villages.

The movement of Santals in Barind was characterised by almost a total absence of arson. Properties belonging to tribals were looted at the initial stage of the movement, perhaps to intimidate the individuals having a different view on the insurgency. With the gradual attainment of solidarity the agitators only looted away standing crop from the fields which had been alienated from the tribals.

---

3. W.J. Culshaw & W.G. Archer : The Santal Rebellion, Man in India, Vol. XXV, December 1945 p. 233

Chapter 6
The Leader

A new polity and leadership grew among the tribals in Barind, as against the traditional leadership which failed to ameliorate the sad plight of the tribe as outlined in the foregoing pages. This new leadership gradually arranged itself in an aggressive posture, projecting a new ideal for the acceptance of the society, in order to achieve a goal. The caste and creed differences were being submerged in the national stream of consciousness directing the entire energy in securing freedom from the foreign yoke. To be with it, it was necessary for the tribals to come out of the shell of defensive stance and join the mainstream. To that end in view, they sought to drown their tribal identity. It is also significant that the new leadership availed of the prevailing circumstances, to focus the aspiration of the ethnic group. Considering from this aspect, Jitu's movement was different and more advanced towards the state formation idea, than that of the Santal insurrection of 1855-56. Under the leadership of Jitu, the tribals had taken fragment of the non-cooperation movement, and the names of Gandhi and Swaraj were invoked several times during the entire process of the movement. Tribal identity was sought to be merged in national identity. Hence tribals in large numbers became Hindus.

It may be recalled that extensive land alienation had led to loss of identification of individuals to particular villages. Alienation of land made many a Santal day-labourers taking refuge in villages where Santals had been living in large homogeneous groups. Such individuals merged their identities with the Santal society and swelled the ranks of the Sannyasi Santals under their leader Jitu.

Jitu Santal alias Jitu Hembram was born in 1883 at Khochakandar in Mangalpura Anchal within Habibpur thana. His father Biram Hembram and mother Tele Murmu had migrated to Khochakander with the first batch of Santals from Santal Parganas (from Saharpur village of Dumka). Dark in complexion, medium built, eyes deep set, broad forehead, Sunken cheek, nose broad and blunt, he was about 5'6" in height. Irrepressible in spirit, he was called the Marang Sardar or the Great Chief. Nothing is known about his early boyhood. But he was born amid spreading cultivation, and as he grew up, the simmering discontent among his fellow-tribals could not have escaped him.

According to Bangi Hembram, the daughter of Jitu he used to get up at early dawn, take his bath and then would sit for his daily worship. He had erected a Kali Temple beside his house- a thatched hut on high plinth. He had about ten bighas of land; the cultivation was looked after by hired workers. Every afternoon, many people used to come at his house; gossips and religious songs (Kirtan) used to continue for hours. Jitu was a member of the Satyam Shibam sect. He himself would not worship the deity. Two maidens - one of them from Khockakander - used to perform worship. Jitu's preceptor was one Buyu Santal. Another old gentleman would come on Tuesdays or on occasions. He was an old Hindu. He had a tiger skin to be used during worships. He was called Thakur Baba by all. After the death of Jitu, he had come once. Arjun was almost inseparable from Jitu.

Jitu did not smoke. On occasions he used to take Ganja (Canabis Indica). He was rather suave in his manners. However unreasonable people would be, Jitu would explain things with utmost patience. Large number of people came who would carry pearl rice for the goddess Kali. Heaps of pearl rice were used to be helped by people themselves. During the childhood of Bangi Hembram Jitu became Hindu. It may be mentioned in passing that Bangi was married at the age of fifteen with Matru Kisku, of Bheluadanga in Gazole thana.

Jitu was a man of very cleanly habits and was punctilious about his appearance. He married four times. At the time of his death, only one of his wives was living. Bangi's mother was the second wife. The son Biram was begotten by his first wife.

Very often, Jitu was carried away to jail. In cases started against him by the administration, Jitu was helped considerably by Shri Nagen Kumar Chakraborty, son of Shri Kashiswar Chakraborty the religious leader, who was also a legal practitioner. On such occasions he would take his flute along. On other times he would carry a sword-stick as well. Bangi remembered that police did not misbehave with Jitu, or create trouble at his house, when they would hold raids. Jitu carried a small brass container with him; he never showed the contents to anybody and had the belief that would protect him from all dangers. His deity was Goddess Kali with whom he talked in his dreams. He used to wear a talisman as well in his right arm by a red thread. During the evening religious recitals, Jitu used to compose songs and sing them. Bangi remembered one such song :

> nun-ah marang dhartire
> manwa chikata bape bujhau
> dariakhan
> shermapuri neaotapa bachha
> jatidharam

(Meaning: in such a wide world, O man, why don't you realise that Divine Rule is your religion!)

To hold evening meetings and religious recitations was to affirm and strengthen conditioned power, on which the power of the leader rested.

During long years of struggle, other songs were composed by Jitu. Bangi remembered the following one:

> maldaha jehelre
> jitu-arjun dokin tolakana
> chandomuni munie menaekhan
> sonamunie raraina

(Meaning : In Malda Jail Jitu and Arjun are detained. If God be for honesty, dearest goddess will release me.)

This was reportedly composed by Jitu when he was in Jail.

Certain interesting features are revealed from the statement of Bangi Hembram. She was eighteen when Jitu was killed in police firing. Three years prior to the incident of Adina she had been married. Conversion of Jitu to Hinduism was effected in her childhood. Jitu might have been converted around 1917. The movements against enhancements had started in 1907 in Gazole area. In 1910, Mr. Vas had settled some such problems. Fresh troubles had sprouted in Habibpur area in 1910, mainly with the Mahadevpur and Porsha Zamindaries. Habibpur had been leavening up, and that is when a youngman of thirtythree or so had changed his religion. Thakur Baba mentioned earlier was none other than Kashiswar Chakraborty. This incident of conversion places him before the Hindu Mission or Hindu Sabha in matters of converting the tribals into Hinduism in Barind. In the District Gazetteer 1969 Mr. J.C. Sengupta mentioned that the Satyam Shibam Sect had come into being in 1905. The similarity in the tenets of the sect with those of the Sapha Hor were striking; the similarity to Brahmo Samaj was, however, very distant. The Santals who had migrated to Barind from the Santal Parganas after 1870 had among them some followers of the Sapha Hor. Later, the precepters of the sect used to visit Barind. As such, not much of resistance from the Santals in matters of conversion was evinced. The mass conversion rather indicated the social will at following a programme. The Santals do not believe in Gurus or spiritual mentors. This system got into the Santal society through the Babajiu sect of the Sapha Hor movement. The statement of Jitu's daughter reveals the affiliation of Jitu to the Sapha Hor through his Guru Buyu Santal. We have already seen that some Hindu tenets were introduced by Bhagrit Baba in the Santal society. Then, what led Jitu to the conversion into Hinduism? The new emerging leadership sought to all prestige of being full-blooded Hindus. That would have been shaking off the societal leadership which was a pre-requisite to consolidate leadership. This large-scale conversion was a thrust from within the tribal society keen to get out of the defensive shell of isolation. In case of the Santals, the idea arose out of rumination after their signal defeat in the insurrection of 1855-56. As mundane failures are apt to be probed in the supernatural, some people came to the conclusion that the tribal Gods had failed the tribe. The instrument of social resilience developed by the Sapha Hor led the tribals on to the next stage of development - the conversion which was a part of the process of social resilience towards a bigger goal, the mundane upliftment. Conversion holds prospect of betterment in mundane affairs. This may partly be attributed to the intense activity of the converts themselves. But conversion to a religion ot the dominant society around holds the prospect of blunting the aggressiveness of that society in the environ. An expectation of enhancing the tolerance-level of the dominant society towards the tribe would also be there. This was important for the tribals groaning under the adverse conditions, for, without alienating the dominant society, a method had to be devised to effect improvement of the situation. All these factors had worked at Barind at the time of conversion of Jitu and his fellow tribals. The extent of this regeneration may be measured from the population out of 72000 Santals (approx.) 4000 were Christian Santals, and the remaining was equally divided between the Hindus and the animists.

Installing goddess Kali as the personal deity can be identified as an endeavour to be different from others in society. It must be remembered that Jitu was a religious leader and religion was used as an instrument in the process of consolidation of his hold over fellow tribals.

According to Shyam Murmu, a disciple of Jitu, religious observances were used as a cover of the movement payment of rents and abwabs. But when the administration imposed restrictions on political meetings, Jitu accepted the advice of Kashiswar Chakraborty to organise more religious meetings and congregations which would enable him to preach his ideas. The preachings enabled him to condition the tribals to the approach of the movement, effecting a sense of solidarity of the tribe.

How did Jitu appear to the Santals in Barind? A song composed by the village bards around the time would allow us a glimpse of him:

> khochakandar jitubaba
> disum disum horem pracharatko,
> mabon mantara satang shibang sundaram
> disum disum horem pracharatko.

(Meaning: O Jitubaba of Khochakandar, you brought the message of Satyam Shibam Sundram to the countrymen through your preachings. You brought the message that Shiba is true, that Rama is true.)

It would appear that Jitu was accepted as a religious preacher by fellow tribals. The philosophical aphorism Satyam Shibam Sundaram had a befitting transformation, may be in the preachings or may be in the comprehension of the tribals, to indicate that Shiba was true as also Rama. This transformation of the real meaning verging on corruption was accepted by the tribals as those ideas kindled the memory of Shiba (an aboriginal deity taken into the Hindu Pantheon) and Rama (with whom the tribal ancestors had gone to Lanka to fight Ravana the Demon King). It may be recalled that Shiba was woven into the myths of the tribe concerning creation: in a variation of the myths it has been given out that the mythical pair of birds landed initially on the matted lock of Shiba spread to accommodate them until Marang Buru created land for them. Rama has not only been mentioned in the Mare Hapramko Reak Katha; since 1871 he was projected as the only God to be worshipped by the tribals by Bhagrit Baba. A steady lore developed around Rama and those are popular in the Barind even today. These lores influenced the tribal mind and conditioned them to ideas projected by their leaders. The ideas were essentially manifestations of attempt at obtaining internal solidarity, which would enable the tribe to undertake external thrust. It is clear from the lores that superiority in rank of the Hindus was acknowledged, and emulation had been attempted thereby, to lift the tribals to the standard of the dominant society.

There is no denying the fact that Jitu the agitator turned into Jitu the preacher, and the second part of his activities helped him to attain the position of a charismatic leader. The lores about Rama were used by him in his preachings.

> remachandwa hohoeda jatidharam debon rafay baba,
> ramchand jatidharam debon rafaya.

(Ram has been calling us. We shall protect our religion).

In his preachings to the tribals, he would urge them to be clean in observances and live like the Hindus. If the Santals lived a better life thereby, there would not be any difference between the Hindus and the Santals. He advised the Santals not to drink Handia or Pachwai, nor to keep pets like pigs, hens etc. He assured the Santals that if they lived a clean life like the Hindus, God would shower His blessings on them. All these tenets were preached by Jitu through songs composed by himself.

> horjanamdo hindudharam dharam duoar-rebon lebet akan,
> Jatibon dishaya dharambon dohoya chandoduarrebon sabudena.

(Meaning: We are Santals, we are Hindus, we shall have to protect our religion. Ram is our Lord, bearing him as such, we shall have to wade through the life. We are His subjects.)

> rajdo rapajdo dishumko repechkan
> naowa dishumdo takoyahkan?
> janamhilahre aristihilahre ram lakashman
> chittan kagachrekin alakat
> naowa dishumdo aliyanhkan.

(Meaning: The kings are fighting for nothing. Even at the time of birth, Rama assured us that this country belongs to us. We are also involving ourselves in unnecessary quarrels; we should pause and think).

Through songs, Jitu used to teach his fellow tribals. His prayer was also through songs:

e satya marang bonga inauba johar
atang tiname.
kalikulauen sarijung hijuhkan dharti
jabad chando gorowaname

(Meaning: O God! Do accept my homilies in your grace. Be with me as long as I live in this world).

Throughout Barind, Jitu held many meetings among the tribals and large number of Santals became Hindus and came within the fold of Satyam Shibam sect. In these meetings, he was invariably accompanied by Arjun. Along with religious preachings, Jitu used to talk about Adina Mosque being one of the abandoned palaces of Ramachandra. In these meetings he also urged upon the tribals and others to stop payment of rents and abwabs to the Zamindars or to the government. The inhospitable area was developed into arable fields by the sweat of the tribals and the tribals have the moral right to enjoy and rule over it. The outcome of these meetings and exhortations was that almost all tribals stopped paying rent. These meetings used to draw considerable crowd. It is reported that Jitu used to hold meeting at Adina every eighth day where thousands of tribals flocked. Through speeches, and moving through places as if on pilgrimage - where Ramachandra had supposedly stayed and moved, he instilled the belief in the minds of the Santals that Adina Mosque was in effect an abandoned palace of Ramachandra where he stayed in exile. Once in a fortnight he used to attend large congregation at Dinajpur, ostensibly to worship Goddess Kali. There was an embargo on political meetings; as such, these went in the name of religious gatherings. Most of these meetings were watched by local police as well. The organisation that Jitu could build up was a cause of worry to the administration.

On the 1st. September 1919, village Khochakandar was described in an official document as a peaceful place with two houses of barber, and a few houses of Santals and Deshis. The people were not litigious. They lived on cultivation and caste professions. Yet, after a decade, this village became the centre of tribal movements. A description of the village on 2nd January 1929, in a state document depicts the place as a centre of all sorts of Santal agitations. Jitu Santal, the leader alias the 'Santal Raj' lived there. Jitu with his lieutenant Arjun Santal of Bijail started a Ryot Samity (Praja Samity) in 1924, with all classes of tenants of this and surrounding villages. Almost all big jotedars and ryots took part in the agitation and stood against the Zamindars and Mahajans. Sageeruddin Sarkar of Noapara and Jitu were then over — lords of the area. Important village- chiefs like Khatibulla Sarkar Hazi, Guroodoyal Sarkar, Keshi Mandal, Chandra Manda, Karful Mandal and others, almost all tenants joined Samity and all stood against the Zamindars and Mahajans who were mercilessly and inhumanly oppressive to the tenants in general. A good amount of money was realised from the tenants on a subscription of annas /4/- per plough. Subsequently, in 1924 there was a misunderstanding among the leaders and the Samity was split in two. Santals went out with their leaders Jitu and Arjun. It dawned on the tribal leaders that their interests were not being considered identical by the rest. From this point of time, Jitu asserted his tribal self and assumed the leadership of the Santals.

According to Shyam Murmu of Khocha Kandar, a living disciple of Jitu, his mentor had started with No Tax Movement. His contention was that they had cleared the jungle and made the land areable; as such it was theirs. The country was theirs and they had the moral right to administer it. The presence of the foreign ruler was essentially irrelevant. As such, Jitu had urged upon people to stop paying rents and abwabs. "Ethnicity, too, was a correlate of class solidarity in some of the nineteenth century peasant rebellions. At one extreme it could be expressed, positively, as a ritual affirmation of the tribal identity of the peasantry involved in an uprising"[1]. Payment of rent to the Zamindars having been stopped Jitu started preaching the 'Santal Raj'. He assured all that in

1. Guha, Ranjit: Elementary Aspects of Peasant Insurgency, p. 173

the Santal Raj, people would not have to pay taxes or abwabs like they were paying to the Zamindars and the government. In the Santal Raj, the land-holders will have to pay only one winnowing fan of paddy for each bigha of land held. There would not be any other tax or impost. If anybody wanted to settle any dispute, a fee of Rs. 1/4/- annas tendered to the chief would get him the desired result. He will not have to run from pillar to post at courts established by the British Raj, nor would he be required to sell his land or bullocks to procure money to reach the pleaders, or clerks at the court. The justice would be dispensed near at hand-in the presence of his chief.

It may be recalled that in the wake of the non-cooperation movement, arbitration Courts were established by the citizens at various places, wherein elected representatives of the locality heard and dispensed social justice by imposing fines or reprimands on the guilty persons. These Courts were set up in a bid to boycott the Courts established by the British Raj. Such system of dispensing social justice has been in vogue among the tribals since long, and even to-day, the tribal Panchayat (More Hor among the Santals) is fairly strong. Abhorrence for the abwabs and similar imposts had all along been marked among the tribals, because that was cutting at the root of their prosperity. Jitu and his lieutenants had earlier contacts with the Swarajists. Around this time Jitu started saying that the British Raj would come to an end soon, to be replaced by the Gandhi Raj which would be beneficial to the poor Santals. Jitu was successful in defining the situations and conveying some kind of symbolic meaning for them.

Against the powerful British Rule backed by the presence of condign power of the army and police, Jitu offered his personality and created an organisation which helped much in the conditioning of the tribals. The Satyam Shibam sect added to his power of conditioning the people. Payment of taxes was stopped by the people at his instance. Simultaneously, Jitu built up a condign power in the Sannyasi Santals. Passive resistance was exercised by not paying taxes and refusing to obey orders of the administration. Whereas Mahatma Gandhi employed an asymmetrical resistance by non-violence, the pattern adopted by Jitu was evidently a symmetrical one. It would be seen later that as Jitu attempted at taking recourse to condign power against condign power, he was vanquished by a superior instrument wielding more power.

In 1924, he secured the free and voluntary support of his tribe. A large number of Santals had collected around him and he had been the guiding star of the Satyam Shibam sect in the Barind. His inseparable lieutenant Arjun of Bijail and others of Habibpur thana were moving from place to place to organise the Santals. In November 1924, the Santals started plundering crops from the fields of others. Cases were instituted at Habibpur and Gazole thanas. The troubles were over an extensive area. The Santals were moving with bows and arrows, and agressively too. These aggressive overtures were essentially acts of conscious violation of the symbols of authority-a revolt against the feudal authority. As such lootings were mostly from plots of land alienated from the Santals. Police did not take very harsh action. Attempt was however made from the administration to subside the tension. Ultimately, while plundering crops at Kendanga, the Santals killed one individual who had tried to resist them. Stern police action compelled the Santals to lie low for the time being. A whispering-campaign was let loose in the area that the Sannyasi Santals- that is what the adherents of Jitu were known-were bent on driving away the Christians, the Muhammadans and other non-Hindu (particularly the non-Hindu Santals) elements from the area. This propaganda had some effect on the movement. A part of energy had to be dissipated in countering the propaganda. The movement thawed down to a low pitch. But the leader had a core of devoted followers who stood by. No rent was paid to the Zamindars. The leader had attained prestige and veneration of the masses, and established himself as the father figure. Subsequent chain of events would show the falsity of the above propaganda or contention that Jitu had only sought to live with the Hindus alone. After declaring independence, he had tried to impress on other elements the necessity of stopping payment of rents to the Zamindars or the government.

Among the Santals the impact of non-cooperation was not limited to Barind alone. In Midnapore, similar activities were noticed under the leadership of Sailajananda Sen. There also the tribals were afflicted by land-alienation. Petition to the government did not bring any relief. In 1921, non-cooperation movement spread in the Jangalmahal of Midnapore under the leadership of Sailajananda Sen of Congress. The movement assured serious proportion in Silda Pargana. People stopped paying rent and started felling trees indiscriminately. Many employees of the Midnapore Zamindari Company were forced to join the movement. Dispute accentuated over possession of the jungle between the tribals and the Zamindars. Both the sides took to violence. About 1000 Santals looted Dahijuri hat in Binapur police station (Midnapore) on the night of 26 January 1922. The spoil was mainly foreign and country made cloth, but extensive damage to property was inflicted. The attempts of Mr. James Peddies, the District Magistrate to effect a compromise between the parties failed. Trouble spread further over a dispute of catching fish, and at the instigation of the noncooperators the tribals went on a series of rampage. They looted fish from tanks, cut down trees in many places in Midnapore and Bankura. Arrested persons were snatched away from the police at many places. Strong police actions and winning over the tribal Manjhies by rewards and other inducements ultimately broke the backbone of the movement there. Sailajananda Sen was sent to jail.[2]

Santals of three police stations in Midnapore gave up drinking pachwai from licensed shops and took to manufacturing it illegally at their own houses. Open hostility was being exhibited towards excise authorities.

A spirit of defiance had taken hold of the tribals elsewhere as well. In Chittagong (now in Bangaladesh), forty three Santal

2. Das, A.K. & S. Mukhopadhyay: Paschim Banger Adibasi Andolan, pp. 57-58.

labourers employed in the Chittagong Municipality struck work from 22 June 1922. The strike was in protest against ill-treatment by the Superintendent, Water Works. The authorities ultimately acceded to the demands of the striking workers and the strike ended on 1st. July 1922.

On 26 December 1921, about 2200 out of a total of 26000 Santal miners employed in the various collieries of Asansol Sub-division struck work, demanding higher wages and other amenities. No apparent cause existed for the strike other than circulation of various unfounded stories and rumours among the labourers. When those rumours ceased to gain ground, the strikers gradually returned unconditionally to work.

In Barind violent overtures gradually came down in 1925. The leader was, however, consolidating his hold over the people. He had drawn himself away from the general stream of movement. The tribal self was asserting Hundreds of tribals would come to see him at his village home, attend the evening religious recitals and go back. To hold evening meetings and religious recitations was to affirm and strengthen conditioned power, on which the power of the leader rested. Plenty of pearl rice and other presents were brought by them to their dear leader. They would partake of the same freely. The Great Chief's prowess cast a spell on them all. He had after all effected a stoppage of paying rent and the obnoxious abwabs to the Zamindars, and shown them the way how to resist coercion and tortuous exactions. His flute and sword-stick assumed a new dimension to the ardent believers. Why! Did not Lord Krishna have the flute and the 'Chakra' (the Sudarshan Disc) with him? And he was a mighty warrior revered as a God. And the Chief talked to the Great Goddess Kali in his dreams. He is protected too by divine grace. The imagination of the tribals had caught fire and it created a halo around their leader Jitu.

The significance of this Krishna motif would be better understood if we recall the processes of conversion of various ethnic groups to Hinduism during the twentieth century. When the Bratya Kshatriyas and the 'Gupta' Kshatriyas were converted, the conversion ceremonies included the ritual sacrifice (Havan) and worship of Lord Parthasarthy. Though it is not known for certain if Kashiswar Chakraborty had done the same thing while converting the Santals, the conversions of Bratya Kshatriya in Dinajpur and Bagurah came to be known to the Santals in Barind. The associated pomp and ceremonies could be possible because the Hindu Mission received financial assistance for each conversion ceremony from the Hindu Sabha. Besides, the Rajbanshies were more affluent. Kashiswar Chakraborty did not have such assistance and his protege were throughly impoverished. The divine attributes of Lord Krishna as represented in the flute and the 'Chakra' were fit for emulation by the warrior in Jitu who had all the love for his tribesmen. And the followers perceived the role of the leader in that light. An aura of greatness was imputed on Jitu by his followers, which is not incompatible to human nature, particularly for a tribe in acute distress trying to find out an exit from the mesh of defensive shell that it had created around itself. The experiences provided by Jitu were strongly satisfying. In him, his followers perceived themselves as better, bigger and more active men. This identification and emulation enabled the tribals to perceive Jitu as a symbolic projection of an ideal, a defiance to authority synonymous to Adharma. The production of culture is a process in which the dominated groups constantly inter-act with the economically and culturally dominant group, selectively borrowing from it and re-interpreting in the light of their perception, and suitability. Culture flows down to the dominated class from the dominating one; reception is expressed in emulation. But the emulated features would be placed in their own way of ordering and interpreting the world.

In 1927, Jitu declared complete Swaraj, became the 'Raja of the country and invited people to come under his 'Raj' where land-holders would have to pay only one winnowing-fan of paddy per bigha of land held. In case of disputes, both civil and criminal a fee of Rs. 1/4/0 only was to be paid. Many Santals became his subjects of their own volition. Almost all stopped paying rent to the landlords.

It may be recalled that many tribals had stopped paying rent even in 1924. The Santals had been living by themselves since then, and the administration did not perhaps take the situation that seriously. After all, the Santals were naturally late in paying off taxes and the arrears took time to be noticed. Jitu and his men were enjoying the benefit of this non-interference of the administration. Then what led to the declaration of independence by Jitu?

We must perceive the impact of veneration of the masses on the leader. The attributes invested on him through social veneration had ascribed power, wisdom and fame into him, to which he reacted to live upto the expectation level of the masses. A programme was the necessity of the hour, to keep the agitated Santals together; a programme that would fetch 'real' power and prestige. This 'power' had a direct relation to the land that the tribals held and was intimately related to their expectations, may hope of the tribals. In declaring independence in 1927 Jitu only reacted to the expectation of his followers.

There was reaction in another quarter as well. The administration took dim view of the tribal declaring 'Swaraj'. The earlier overtures were passed off as ripples of the non-cooperation movement which had hardly touched the district. In 1927, the reckoning was different. The Santals had deliberately stopped paying rent-not out of indigence, but in pursuance to a definite programme. Under order of the district administration, a prosecution was initiated against Jitu and Arjun under bad-livelihood clauses. Non F.I.R. Prosecution No. 2 dated 11th April 1927 under Sections 110/118 Criminal Procedure Code, Emperor vs. Jitu Santhal- had the following against the accused:

> "The accused is a habitual
> cheat and extortioner and is
> so desperate and dangerous
> as to render him being at
> large without security hazardous
> to the community and so he

> was run down u/s 110 Cr.P.C.
> and was convicted."

On 21st June 1927, Jitu was ordered under Sections 110/118 Cr. P.C. to execute a bond of Rs. 500/- with two sureties of the like amount to be of good behaviour for a period of two years. Similar order was passed against Arjun. These orders were passed by Mr. M.M.Ghosh the Sub-divisional Officer and were subject to confirmation by the learned Sessions Judge at Malda Court. The learned Sessions Judge applied his judicial mind in the matter and did not eventually confirm the orders passed by the Sub-divisional Officer. Both Jitu and Arjun were acquitted.

Meanwhile the Santals wanted to worship Goddess Kali at Malda. The administration did not favour the idea. At the place of worship, a large assembly of Santals might spell trouble for the administration. So, an order under Section 144 Criminal Procedure Code was passed restraining the Santals from assembly. The district administration also barred the entry of Kashiswar Chakraborty in Malda district by an order, as it was reckoned that he had been instigating that Santals against the administration. The Santals did not like the order at all. They flouted the order of the administration and performed the worship of Goddess Kali on the 8th May 1927. About 3000 Santals collected and participated in the worship, and the festivities ended peacefully, much to the relief of the administration which eventually did not interfere with the celebrations.

This acquiesing of the administration in matters of the Kali Puja and the subsequent striking down of order of the Sub-divisional Officer by the learned Sessions Judge had an exhilarating effect on the tribals. Their faith on the prowess and wisdom of Jitu was confirmed. He was elevated to the status of the charismatic leader. His mandates ran through the area among Santals without any question being raised. The credulity of the Santals was a reaction to the leader's providing a satisfying experience unto them, showing them the way to the promised state. The superior wisdom imputed upon him by the masses through veneration had more than been justified.

Around this time, an area of 104 square miles of Habibpur thana and Bamangola thana was surveyed by the air survey methods. Because of technical questions of verification, the experimentation was postponed in other areas of Malda district. This was the first occasion on which 16" mapping was carried out in India from air-photographs. In the winter of 1927 and the spring of 1928, by using an Eagle Aircraft Camera holding a negative 7" x 7" and capable of 100 exposures, actual photography was carried out in Habibpur and Bamangola. The plane flew at a height of about 6000 ft. While the photographs were being taken, the entire area was divided in strips running north and south, so that on completion of one strip, the machine could turn and take up the next strip without delay. The operations continued till April 1928, covering a total of 800 square miles, when clouds and poor visibility made it impossible to continue.

Flying machines were rare objects in 1927. The plane hovering above like a big bird might have reminded the ardent tribals of Garuda, the mighty carrier of Lord Vishnu. Or, it might have been suggested by Jitu himself to his followers-the chronicle attributes the idea to Jitu-that Lord Vishnu might have visited the area. Miracles are concomitant to charisma. Jitu had by then become a charismatic leader and whatever he said was accepted by his followers. So the tribals believed in the miracle of the visit of Lord Vishnu on his divine carrier Garuda

In the chronicle, the credulilty of the Santals has been obliquely mentioned. Of course, to any discernible reader, this queer assertion of Jitu, or the belief of his followers, would seem almost grotesque. But this will surely show the depth of their belief and faith in the leader whose utterances had almost assumed the status of articles of faith, and no less. Yet this phenomenon is not unique to the tribals. People eagerly waiting for the liberator do cherish such ideas verging on the miracle, as would the story of Krishna reveal. In recent times, in April 1922, a rumour was in circulation in Darjeeling district that Gandhiji had vanished from jail leaving only his 'dhoti' behind. In Mymensing district, it was widely circulated that Gandhiji had caused a message to be inscribed on caladium leaves that he had been whipped in jail. People in hundreds were seen examining those leaves. (Gandhiji was arrested and lodged in jail in March 1922).

In January 1922, a rumour was in wide circulation in Rangour district that Imam Mahdi the Saviour of the Musalmans, had been born and would take up the cause of the Khilafat. The ignorant and credulous country folks, especially the Muhammadans, reportedly believed the story implicity. Rumours are harbingers of charismatic leaders as well, and are the first signs of people's acceptance of the leader as such. This is particularly so during a period of expectancy. From the side of the leader, there was yet another reason. He had succeeded in raising a hope in the minds of his tribal brethren—a hope to live with. He himself had been enjoying the support of his tribe. They had been working on instructions till then: the rents stopped, people in arms ready to react to any threat. He had devised a programme. There had been mass conversion, people progressing in a particular direction and they had established their Raj. What next?

The severe drought in 1927 had marred the prospect of any crop in the mono-crop Barind. No assistance from the administrtion came, and the agonising thought of the coming days had been unnerving to all. The programme of Swaraj was proceeding as anticipated, but to do something for the masses was an imperative. The fire kindled must not be allowed to be put off by pangs of hunger. Hope must be revived-hope in the supernatural powers of the leader, hope in the grace of God, which must continue till some more programmes could be devised, till better days dawned. Hence the pronouncement that Lord Vishnu had visited Barind on his divine carrier Garuda. Krishna was an incarnation of Lord Vishnu on earth, and in the reckoning of the tribals, Jitu had the attributes of

Krishna. No incompatibility appeared to the tribal which had come to believe in his leader.

In September 1928, the followers of Jitu started plundering crops from the fields. They disobeyed the orders issued by the Civil as well as the Criminal Courts asking them to desist from such activities. Situation became very grave; several cases were started against Jitu and his men. About 100 Santals were arrested from the Doba and sent to jail. The situation was brought under control by deploying armed forces in the Barind. Chargesheets were submitted in many cases. Intensity of raids for offences under the Excise Act was accelerated in the Barind. Prosecutions under Section 46(a) of Excise Act were submitted in large number, ending in conviction. The usual punishment for such offences was fine ranging between Rs. 7/- and Rs. 15/-, in default rigorous imprisonment for a week or a fortnight. To the Santals the latter was welcome, because in many cases they had not the ability to pay at all.

The administrative actions against the Santals effected a temporary lull in their activities. No major incident took place during 1929 and 1930. Needless to say that, more Santals lost their lands in ex-parte decrees. The bumper crop of 1930 was taken as a grace of god though there was much pressure from the government Tehsildars to pay up arrear loans. The Santals had noted with gloom that while the rest of the district was receiving assistance for seeds and weeding, and Test Relief with Gratuitous relief, the Santals in Barind were being pressed for arrear loans and taxes. In view of occasional resistance from the Santal the loan-collectors did not venture to disturb the hornet's nest. In 1931 another programme was set by Jitu. He started collecting subscriptions from people of the locality ostensibly to establish Gandhi Bank. Subsequent inquiries indicated that Jitu was collecting money to procure and distribute 'charkhas' (spinning wheels) to the tribals. This was in pursuance to the call given by Gandhiji to take to the charkha. Jitu himself had started wearing khadi by that time. In fact, from 1921 onwards charkhas were being procured and used by people in almost all districts; it was a part of programme of boycotting foreign goods. In some parts of Malda also, the charkha was in use among Hindus and Muslims. For Jitu and the Santals necessity ordained the taking up of the programme.

Whatever might be the real intent of Jitu, a case was started against him, Gopal Santal of Kokabirni and Ragad Santal of Tulshidanga, on the complaint of Biju Mandal of Singhpara and others. (Habibpur Police Station Case No. 6 dated 13.6.1931 under Sections 420/120B IPC). The complaint was that Jitu and his associates had cheated the complainant and others in respect of cash money, by realising money as petition fee, by falsely inducing the people to believe that they would get loan from Gandhi Bank without interest. The case was investigated and chargesheet was submitted against Gopal Santal, Ragad Santal, Arjun Santal of Bijail and Rinchi Santal of Kalaibari, to stand trial at court. Arjun and Rinchi died in jail in December 1931 before the trial was even taken up. Gopal and Ragad were acquitted. Jitu Santal and others could not be sent up in chargesheet for want of sufficient evidence. The witnesses in this case were Biju Mandal, Dhana Mandal, Mirza Mandal and Kandan Mandal, all residents of village Singpara.

In yet another case, a similar accusation was brought by the administration against Jitu and one of his associates. The incident summary was that, on 5th Magh 1337 BS, Mathur Poli and others of Jaypura, on getting information that Gandhi loans were being distributed on payment of Rs. 1/- per head by Jitu Santal of Khochakandar, went to him. They saw many persons paying Rs. 1/-per head to one Bhuban Mohan Dey of Mothabari (in Kaliachak thana). Bhuban had been staying at the house of Jitu at that time. Jitu had reportedly induced people to believe that by such payment they would get Gandhi loans without interest. Mathur and his companions also paid Re.1/- each for the loan. Later, Mathur learnt that they had been cheated by Jitu by misrepresentation. Jitu did not refund the money on demand; so Habibpur Police Station Case No. 1 dated 6.7.1931 under Sections 420/120 B Indian Penal Code was instituted, and on investigation, chargesheet was submitted against Jitu and Bhuban Mohan Dey. Both the accused persons were, however, acquitted on trial on 19.1.1932, for want of sufficient evidence. In this case, Mathur Poli, Daksha Poli, Batu Poli, Jalha Poli, Dialu Poli and Jogendra Poli, all of Jaypura,· deposed against Jitu and Bhuban.

Barind was an easy place to make quick money. As it is, money was a scarce commodity to the Santals. The alienation of land, taxes, expenditure on account of cases and the general poverty had made the Santals dependent on loans. These loans had been eroding the ground they were standing on due to accumulation of interest at extortionate rates. During the movement sponsored by Jitu and his brethern from 1924 the Santals had stopped paying rent to the Zamindars, but sustenance had all along been difficult in the monocrop areas. The illiterate Santals had no notion of banks. The loan from Gandhi Bank had turned out to be a hoax-for instead of money, 'charkhas' were assured. Money was a dire necessity to the Santals, and outsiders played on the theme and made money themselves out of it, by cheating the poor Santals. Md. Habibullah, Devendranath Gupta and Gopal Chandra Choudhuri- three enterprising adventurers came down to Gopalnagar in Habibpur thana from Englishbazar thana area and lured many a Santal in parting with Rs. 2/4/- and 10 seers of paddy each, with the assurance that loans between Rupees two lakhs and Rupees four lakhs would be floated shortly in Barind whereby the subscribers would be given priority in matters of loan. Gopal Choudhuri posed himself as a big Mahajan. However, after cheating a hundred or so tribals, they were found out by the police who forthwith started a criminal case (Habibpur Police Station Case No. 4 dated 19.5.1932 under Sections 420/120 B IPC). The accused persons were tried at Court and convicted.

Collection of subscription with one pretext or the other was not a unique feature in Barind. A number of funds had been opened around 1921, throughout the country, on the eve of the initiation of the non-cooperation and the khilafat movements.

In almost all the districts of Bengal, collections were raised for the Khilafat fund. Malda district was not an exception. Subsequently, Tilak's Swarajya Bhandar (fund) was initiated by students who had joined the national school movement; 25 per cent of the collection was to be sent to the Provincial Committee. Subsequently, other funds viz. Smyrna Fund, Ankora Fund, Aeroplane Fund and many others appeared in the scene. In peaceful interludes between one movement and the other, volunteers were raising funds in districts. Funds were raised by the Hindu Sabha as well to help the conversion ceremonies held at various places. It is not that the volunteers had been immaculate on all occasions in respect of the money thus collected.

Apart from such group-collection of funds, individual adventurers sought to gain by the process. An example may be cited, which would clarify the position as to how some individuals fished in troubled water.

In November 1922, a paper note similar in design and size to the five rupee currency note, headed "The Bond of Islamic Unity, (Unlimited)" and with an inscription in Guzrati to the effect that the purchaser would receive Rs. 10,000 when Swaraj was attained, was being sold at Titagar in 24-Parganas district for annas two. Khilafat volunteers were asked to stop selling of those Bonds which were not being sold by regular volunteers. On 30 November 1922 two Khilafat volunteers were arrested on Strand Road, Calcutta for creating disturbance when they were quarrelling with a man who was selling the Bonds. They were fined Rs. 5/- each, in defalut, one day's simple imprisonment. Another volunteer was arrested at Bhowanipore on the same charge; he was let off with admonition.

The programme of collecting funds to distribute charkhas was undertaken by Jitu rather late. It is quite possible that the collection went in the name of Gandhi and the prospect of getting interest-free loan was a lure to the cultivators. In effect, the programme was a necessity for the tribal leadership, to keep the flame of resilience alive. Succumbing to the pressures of the administration would have brought an end to the movement of the Santals in Barind, like it happened in Midnapore in 1924. The endeavour of the local administratin had been to rope in Jitu in criminal cases, but it never succeeded. The Santals would not depose anything against him. The last two cases were instituted by Polis which eventually failed. But these cases helped in removing Jitu and other important leaders of the movement away from the scene for sometime; a temporary period of lull would follow to be terminated by another series of events or incidents to keep up the tension in the area. Throughout the area, troubles continued unabated. Other villages in Barind were also seething with unrest. The Santals of village Kuladanga and its neighbouring villages were also sharing the extreme views of Jitu. All the landed properties of almost all the Santals were sold away, or decrees obtained to dispossess them for debts of varying degrees. The Santals were, however, determined to retain possession, ever by force, over these plots. Loosely, these people were also called Sanyasi Santals belonging to Jitu's group; and determined not to obey the orders of the Munsif, Magistrate or the police. They had been trained in keeping, and shooting, bows and arrows. On 10th November 1931, there was a fracas between the agents of the Shah Zamindars of Porsha and the Santals of Kulandanga and Gopalnagar where the Santals made use of their bows and arrows without fearing the gun of the opposite side.

Amin Shah, Zamindar of Porsha had purchased land measuring 448 bighas in auction from Malda Court. His men came to take possession of the land. On 10.11.1931 a rioting took place in which Bhakta Santal, Bharat Santal, Barka Santal, Jagu Santal, Bagat Santal and others of Kulandanga attacked the Zamindar's men with bows and arrows and injured one Khalil Biswas. Abdul Fate Shah of Porsha (Zamindar) residing at Kuladanga Kamat (farm-house) fired several rounds from his gun, with buckshots, causing injuries to one Magat Santal. The Santals dispersed. A case was started against the Santals, arrests were made and within a month, the case ended in chargesheet against the Santals. On 29th November 1931, a prayer was submitted by police before the Court requesting orders restraining the Santals from entering the land in question. So that the Santals did not indulge in riotous activities many of them were prosecuted under Section 107 Criminal Procedure Code (Non-F.I.R. Prosecution No. 12/1931). The Santals lost the land in the long run.

1931 ended without any other major incident.

Independence was declared by Jitu in 1927 and his followers had brought about a charisma around him. They were following his mandates of not paying taxes to the Zamindars. But loss of land through Court-sale was also a reality, and dealt serious blows on the 'Raj'. So long, Jitu had been a Great Chief or Marang Sardar. The control over his men, and to some extent on others in the Barind had been accomplished; the sway on a geographical area had also been established. To Jitu, the consolidation of this achievement needed the sacramental and ritualistic support to elevate himself to the position of the real 'Santal Raj'. The 'Raj' was also dependent upon a historical and traditional association. The immanent intelligence directing the social change required a boost in formalising the status. Upto this point of time, Jitu had been a tribal leader, but not a king. The charismatic leader had the necessity of continuing a state of anxiety which was complementary to his scheme. A group had been brought about and it had been working together for common ends. The formalisation of the agency to deal with the outstanding external relationship of his group of men working in Barind had to be accomplished as well.

Leaders affect the followers. But they are also affected by the veneration of the followers. The masses attribute unto the leaders some qualilties. Those in turn, influence the leaders, who react upon the masses in such a manner as to increase their power so that they fit in with the image created for them. The masses carry the culture within which the special functions of leadership rest. In any field touching the mores or folkways intimately, leadership must fall in line with what the masses hold to be true. The Golden Era of Champa had been notionally re-created. The Santal mind had the dream of attaining power' through the 'Raj' as conceived by them and enunciated by their leader. And the leader, in turn, was forced to undertake the perilous trail.

On 3.12.1932, Jitu sent Ram Santal of Banshihari (Dinajpur) to occupy the Adina Mosque within Gazole thana, fit enough to be the capital of the new 'Raj'.

Chapter 7

The Culmination

The imposing ruins of the Adina Mosque lay within the Barind at Gazole thana, near Hazrat-Pandua, the erstwhile capital of the Sultans of Bengal. It was no longer in use as a mosque, for prayer and congregation, and had been taken over by the Archaeological Department as a 'protected place' of ancient glory. The huge building lay within the reach of the Santals, open almost on all sides, displaying the past splendour of royalty. It had earlier 378 minarets. The Badshah-ki-Takht or the seat of the emperor lay on twentyone pillars. Ten thousand people could congregate there at a time without any difficulty. This mosuqe was built by Sekender Shah in 770 Hijri (1369 A.D.) and the materials used had been collected from Hindu temples or Buddhist shrines by demolishing those. Even today, indelible mark of Hindu gods or Buddhist ritualilstic signs are discernible on the mosque. Some scholars are of the opinion that the mosque was built upon the ruins of a Buddhist monastery [1]. All the scholars are, however, unanimous on the point that the materials for construction of the mosque were collected from Hindu temples and Buddhist shrines. The laymen of the area did not feel perturbed over such technical problems; they were context with associating the structure with the Hindu religion or with Hindu rule in one way or the other. The residual remainings of Hindu religious insignia or idols were convincing enough to them.

The origin of the word Adina also added to the controversy among scholars. The similarity between 'Adina' and 'Adinath' led many to guess that the mosque was originally a temple of Lord Shiva of the Hindu pantheon. Dr. Pradyot Ghosh of Malda College thinks that the connotation of Adinath as lord Shiva was an outcome of Jain influence. But Adina did not reveal any Jain influence at all. Earlier, Adinath had been used

---

1. Chakraborty, Rajani Kanta: Gaurer Itihas, p. 37

to mean God, Parabrahama, Brahmandapati, Paramatma, Narayan, Vishnu, Mahadev, Brahma, the Sun etc. According to Dr. Ghosh, the word Adina had been derived from the Arabic word 'Dani' meaning near or neighbouring. As the mosque was built near to the newly constructed capital of Pandua on the eastern bank of the Mahananda in 1339 AD by Hazi Elias Shah, so it was known as Adina [2]. Be it as it may, in the backdrop of Hindu resurgence, Adina was associated with the Hindus, and the belief was bolstered by the presence of Hindu pieces of idols or religious signs.

To the Santals, the mosuqe meant something more. The Badshah-ki-Takhat was the seat of the king, and where else would it be more befitting for a new king to take seat at the time of coronation. The citadel-like building inspired a sense of royal grandeur; the mimbar (pulpit) stood apart from the Badshah-ki-Takht whence the Imam used to conduct prayers. This mimbar of black basalt has a canopy atop, with Hindu royal insignia. Seven flights of stairs from the floor takes one to the pulpit which is 5'10" in height inside. One of the stairs is adorned with geometrical designs. According to Abid Ali, it was a throne of some Hindu king ; Dr. P. Ghosh disagrees here also-with no good reason. That the throne was bearing indelilble Hindu signs, nobody would disagree, and that the mimbar has the construction of a throne nobody disputes. It is significant that the Santals picked this up as the 'throne' of the 'Santal Raj' and did not choose the Badshah-ki-Takht. The throne commanded view over three sides inside the premises while the back has been blocked by high-wall. The inner courtyard measures 507-1/2 ft. from north to south, and 285-1/2 ft. in the east-west. The whole area was surrounded by wall, dividing the inner premises in 108 Squares with separate minarets. There were 378 minarets in all. The perimeter wall is about 20 ft. high; many of the arches have crumbled down, making it superfluous to use the narrow entrances on the east. The open courtyard was suitable for assembly. In the tribal mind, to win the citadel would have been an achievement. The

2. Ghosh, P.K. : The Architecture of Gour-Vanga, Vol. I, pp 41-42.

Hindus had reigned for centuries-to be replaced by Muslims on conquest, and the British later. Over the ruins, a new kingdom would flourish, a Hindu kingdom revived, having centuries of tradition looking upon them in bliss.

The public mind was conditioned through the lores on Rama. And the lores were connected with Adina Mosque through the presence of a Nagra or a big drum of copper with two copper sticks to play thereon. Santals carry Nagra or such drums during their annual hunt or during Shakrat festival. They also play on the same during dance sessions at Baha, Sohrai or Shakrat. The Nagra is also played on when the Naeke enters the village after performing worship of the Jahar Bongas at Jahar Than during Baha festival. The presence of such a Nagar at Adina Mosque, reportedly seen by the Santals, made them claim the mosque as a place associated with the Santals. It was given out that the Muslims might have changed it into a mosque when they had been ruling. As in the Ramayana, Rama of the Santal lores was the son of king Dasaratha of Ayodhya. He had gone away in exile in the forests with brother Lakshman and wife Sita. Once during their sojourn they had taken shelter under a tamarind tree. It was raining hard, but the exiles did not have a single drop of rain-water on them. In those days, tamarind leaves were large and flat. Those leaves did not allow the rain-water to drop on Rama and his companions. At this, Rama was annoyed - they had come to the forest to suffer and the leaves did not allow them to : So Rama shot an arrow at the tree, and since then, the tamarind leaves were reduced greatly in size. But Rama decided that henceforth they should live in open ground. But, by the grace of god, palaces would have sprung whereever Rama Lakshman-Sita would stay. The Santal lorist says-

ram lakshman bidesh
bharat chatur rajaho
janhirayachhe rama lakshman
tahiretwa jodana garhe ho
tahireto ajodanagare

(Meaning : When Ram-Lakshman were banished, Bharat-Shatrughna became kings. But whereever Rama-Lakshman went, Ayodhyapuri was built up there. So staying therein in new palaces all the time, Rama-Lakshman would go out hunting by beating out the drum).

So, the abandoned palace of Rama with the drum is associated with the Santals. It was from such a palace that the wicked Ravana stole away Sita when Ram-Lakshman had gone out hunting.

ramdo lakshmando sendrakin chalaoen
sitakin bagiade duoarare
sendrakhon hechkate sitakin inelekan
sitato niyegel rabanraja

Thereafter, Rama went to Lanka with many aborigines and rescued Sita after killing Ravana in war.

The above was the strain of conditioning of the Santals in the Barind and adjoining places. A tribal version of Adina incident has to say that Jitu had occupied the Adina Mosque as one of such palaces where Rama had lived during his exile. When the officials had told him that the building was a mosque and in keeping of the government, Jitu had replied that during the Mughal period, the building might have been converted into a mosque, but surely it was an ancient palace belonging to Ramachandra of yore, and that he would not leave the same.

In his preachings to the Santals, Jitu stressed that Adina Mosque was in realilty one of the palaces of Ramachandra who had lived therein during his sojourn in exile, and Satghara, Lusisar, Matikata, Chandbel, Jorabundh etc. were sacred places where gods abound. Jitu and Arjun held many meetings at those places which are in the neighbourhood of Adina. The song composed by Jitu on the score is as follows :-

adina ram-lakshman pandwa chhitakapra
satghara lusisar matikata chandbel
ram-lakshman jorabundh hesahbare butare
jitu arjun sabha uthalo

masebon rarha satang shibang sundaram
dahay shiba sundaram satya bhagaban.

It may be observed how Jitu developed into a charismatic leader, combining the temporal aspect of leadership with the spiritual, as he continued preaching. Earlier we had noticed in case of sido-kanhu how they had combined these two aspects of leadership in them to take up total leadership of the tribe.

Upto 1924, Jitu had been a tribal leader, trying to cultivate the leaders of other dominant communities in the environ, to make a common cause against the Zamindars mainly. During this period, he had engendered a social change by mass-conversion and building up hope among the tribals of reviving the Golden Era of Champa. While projecting a hope for the future, he had consolidated his leadership over the tribals. When the split in the Praja Samity took place he asserted his tribal entity and had a phalanx of solid tribal support behind him. As he assumed the leadership of the tribals, they attributed charisma in him. To sustain the compulsions of social pressure on the leader, he had to effect the continuance of a state of tension and anxiety in the tribe by providing guidelines in consonance with the hope generated; the spirit of his followers had also caught fire. Even when in 1927 he had declared Swaraj, Jitu was no more than a Great Chief (Marang Sardar). The repressive measures taken by the government in the following years had to be countered by him. He had attained power in the localilty, the movement was fairly strong in which the Santals were gaining by not paying rent and other abwabs, but this power was not attended by prestige that ensures continuity of power emanating from the king. Prestige depended on association with objects of traditional and historical standing. He could have built his citadel at Khochakandar; but that would not have fetched the reverence of all, being devoid of any historical or traditional placement. Of course, the resources of a poor tribal leader was in no way sufficient to build up a pucca house even. An innovation does never receive the deference paid to a historical citadel which effects a continum projecting authority. Adina Mosque provided the grandeur, the historical association.

The task of finding appropriate task for the followers developes on the leader. So, in December 1932 Jitu sent his men under the leadership of Ram Santal of Banshihari to occupy Adina Mosque. This sending of a subordinate leader for the task was tantamount to sending the general to take hold of the citadel - a crude emulation of an act of conquest.

Chapter 8

The Battle

One Budhrai Santal of Singra along with Sona Santal of Biswanathpur, Gangarampur thana (District Dinajpur-presently in West Dinajpur), Dukha Santal of Mander in Kharagpur thana (district Monghyr, Bihar); Terka Santal of Bhabuk, Parbat Santal of Sapbalidanga, Mangla Soren of Shershadanga, Lakshman Santal of Dharmapur in Malda thana; Bhairo Santal of Madrail, Dukha Santal of Khantipur, Mohan Kisku of Karchandanga in Gazole thana area; Mongal Besra of Chandipur, Ganesh santal of Habibpur, Rama Santal of Kadamatali, Fuchu Santal of Gopalpur, Mona Santal of Heyatpur, Chhotka Santal of Joydanga, in Habibpur thana area, and many other Santals of different places appeared in Adina and occupied the mosque. The mosque was not in use and was in the custody of the Archaeological Department for preservation as a monument under the Indian Monuments Act. The perimeter wall had crumbled down at many places, bare columns standing in the open. The Badshah-ki-Takht appeared as a dark recess and the throne-like mimbar stood in isolation commanding a view of the open courtyard. The Santals came in large numbers on the 3rd December 1932 and set up one Ram alias Sona Santal, an ex-convict of Banshihari (Dist. Dinajpur), on the throne and declared that they had recaptured the mosque and re-established the lost Hindu kingdom of Pandua. Sona Santal styled himself as Gandhi and addressed the assembled men from the throne-like mimbar. Assuming the name of Gandhi while ascending the throne was also not a unique thing for the Santals. For a long time since 1921, Gandhi was invoked on many occasions by the freedom fighters. Even on 12th January 1922, a Swaraj thana was opened in Rangpur district under an individual who styled himself as Gandhi Darogah. Thereafter, a series of meetings was held with the Santals of Dinajpur, Monghyr, Habibpore Bamongola and the locality as also with the Polis, and other depressed classes. In these meetings, the leaders were urging the listeners not to pay tax in any form. It was declared that the British Rule had come to an end and Gandhiji's Rule had descended, and all should rally round to strengthen the Hindu Kingdom thus revived. All non-Hindus were scrupulously excluded, in that they were not admitted within the premises even. The local Muslims were excited, and brought it to the notice of Maulavi Afazuddin, the Circle Inspector of Police on the 5th December, 1932. The Inspector paid a visit to Adina Mosuqe and with the help of one Sub-Inspector of Police of Gazole thana, could eventually persuade Sona Santal, the so called king, to come down from the throne. But the Santals remained encamped within the mosque-premises. Word was sent to the district headquarter at Englishbazar and on the 6th December, the District Magistrate and the Superintendent of Police talked to the Santals and succeeded in persuading them to leave the mosque. This could be achieved without applying any force.

The Santals left Adina and the leader was touched to the quick. By responsibility of upholding the standard automatically fell on the leader. It was under his instructions that Sona was sent to Adina with the members of the Satyam Shibam Sect. Sona having failed, it was Jitu who was obliged to take the lead himself. The edifice that he was building up would largely depend on the success of the mission of securing unto him a throne fit enough for re-establishing the lost Hindu Kingdom. In this regard, it may be mentioned that as the leader leads his people, he is also subject to the beliefs and wishes of his followers. The glamour that Jitu had attained by long and sustained work, had to be put to test. It was a matter of survival for him. And Jitu acted in a predictable manner. With great fanfare, he went to Adina Mosuqe on 13 December, 1932 and recaptured it. About 500/600 Santals had accompanied him on the occasion. The Santals were armed with farsas, swords, bows and arrows and lathies. The District Magistrate and the Superintendent of Police with armed forces came rushing there with some Zamindars and influential men from the town. They tried their best to persuade the Santals to leave the place. But the Santals did not pay heed to the officials. It is learnt from Shri Shyam Murmu of Khochakandar, a disciple of Jitu that it was proposed to Jitu that a temple for him would be constructed near Pakuahat at government cost and 50 bighas of land would be given to him by formal registration, if he left Adina Mosque alone. It was not proper for him to occupy it. Jitu had reportedly replied that he had not been doing anything for his individual gain, and the proposal would be acceptable if government gave land to all the tribals. The District Magistrate declared the assembly to be unlawful and ordered the arrest of the leaders whereupon the Santals attacked the police. It was three in the afternoon. A constable was wounded with an arrow and subsequently died, while another constable was wounded on the head with a sword by Jitu Santal. Police opened fire and four Santals including Jitu Santal, were killed and four were injured; sixteen Santals including the injured persons were arrested. Of the injured Santals two died at hospital later. A criminal case (Gazole P.S. Case No. 1 dated 13.12.1931 u/s 147/148/353/326 IPC) was started against the Santals and the 16 Santals named above were convicted u/s 147 IPC and were made to sign bonds to keep peace for three years after release, u/s 106 Cr.P.C.

Accounts vary greatly on what happened at Adina Mosque on 13.12.32. The daughter of Jitu narrated the incident with emotion in her voice. According to her, Jitu had come to Adina Mosque to ascend the throne, to be the king. A Santal woman was also brought there to officiate as the Queen. The king is incomplete in the throne without a queen beside him. The Superintendent had assured Jitu that a pucca house would be built for Jitu at Pakua and that an area would be marked out where he would be allowed to hold sway. He explained to Jitu that Adina Mosque being a monument preserved by the government should not be occupied by Jitu. But Jitu did not agree to the proposal. He refused to recognise the District Magistrate and the Superintendent saying that there was no government other than that of Gandhi-there was Gandhi Raj in place of the British Raj and that he would ascend the throne at Adina. As Jitu had been ascending the throne, from the steps he looked back over his shoulder and it was at that time that he was shot at his forehead. He collapsed down to the earth.

In another account, it is held that as Jitu was arguing with the Magistrate, the latter's gaurd addressed him in abusive terms whereupon Jitu drew out his sword-stick; he was then shot from close range.

The third account is that Jitu was sitting atop the throne when he ws asked to come down to talk to the Superintendent which he refused. The Superintendent threatened him when Jitu brought out his sword-stick and was about to pounce on the Superintendent when he was shot down.

The idea prevalent in many circles in the district gives out another version. That Jitu was either atop the throne or was just ascending it, there was no doubt. It was beyond any scope for Jitu to inflict any injury on either the Magistrate or the Superintendent from there.

The throne is about eight feet high from the ground level, and the officials were not definitely standing at the foot of stairs leading upto the throne. What could a man, even with a sword-stick do to the officials? In subsequent police firing four Santals were injured, and on the other side, one constable received arrow-shot injuries on his person. Subsequently, another constable had received head injury from a sword. These clearly indicate that, at the initial state of the fray, the two parties were at a distance from each other, and at the later stage they had closed on each other. It was given out by this version that police did not open fire at the initial stage. When Jitu was ascending the throne, he had looked back over his shoulders when Abul Hayat Khan Chaudhuri the Zamindar of Kotwali fired the shot aiming at him, dropping him dead. Khan Chaudhuri was a skilled hunter and had accompanied the officials from Malda. This version, however, does not find support in any of the official versions over the incident. In all the official versions, it has been reported that police had opened fire at the Santals, killing Jitu and three others. Even in the criminal case, Abul Hayat Khan was kept out of the picture.

The sombre version of the Report on the Police Administration in the Bengal Presidency for the year 1932, under head rioting, was that 'in the Malda district, some Hindu Santhals armed with bows, arrows and other weapons forcibly occupied the Adina Mosque, which is preserved under the Preservation of Ancient Monuments Act, and refused to leave it alleging that it was an old Hindu temple, as it contained relics of many Hindu images. The District Magistrate and the Superintendent of Police, accompanied by some local gentlemen, arrived at the spot with an armed police force. The Santals, who could not be induced to leave the place, became furious and began to discharge showers of arrows and their leader attacked the Superintendent of Police, whereupon the District Magistrate ordered the police to open fire. Two constables, one of whom subsequently died, received serious wound; while three Santhals were killed on the spot and of the three who were injured, two succumbed to their injuries afterwards[1].

It is true that the followers of Jitu were armed but had they taken the aggressive part at the initial stage, there would not have been the occasion of verbal exchanges between Jitu and the officials; nor would there be the occasion of bringing out of the sword-stick by Jitu to assault either the Magistrate or the Superintendent. It follows reason that the officials had taken the decision and shot at Jitu- be it Abul Hayat Khan or a constable-and the Santals replied with arrows. During chase, the other constable might have received injury on his head. There is no doubt that the officials had resorted to violence first. However, the blow was decisive. The Santals fled before the armed constabulary.

Yet in another account furnished by Francis Hopna Hembram the responsibility of occupying the mosque at Adina

1. Craig, T.J.A., Report on the Police Administration in the Bengal Presidency for the year 1932, p. 19

was thrust on one Saona Mardi (Saona Mardi has been noted as 'Sona Mardi' in official records.) of village Biswanthpur, Gangarampur Police Station in Dinajpur district. Saona came to see Jitu at Khochakandar on 30 November 1932. Jitu was working at his kitchen garden and came out to meet the visitor. Saona accosted Jitu as to why he had kept the idol of Kali at his house - the goddess that does nothing but devour human beings, the goddess that sports strings of human heads as garland around herself. It was certainly not wise of Jitu to worship such a goddess; given the opportunity she would devour Jitu one of these days. Saying all these, Saona uttered some incantations and threw some mustard seeds on Jitu. Instantaneously, Jitu became 'possessed'. He took out the Kharga (sacrificial sword) and severed the head of the image of Goddess Kali. Blood started spurting out of the beheaded image of the Goddess. Jitu quietened after some time, and Saona advised Jitu on various matters and took him out to occupy the Adina Mosque. Saona assured Jitu that after occupying Adina Mosque, they would light the sacrificial fire there. On that day, a meeting was scheduled to be held at Adina, to be addressed by Jitu, and many tribals had turned up. As police was there as well, Jitu did not venture to occupy Adina on that day and went to Dharampur where he held meetings on three consecutive days. After three days, Saona again told Jitu to make a move and occupy Adina Mosque. Jitu could not disoblige Saona and agreed. A marriage between Saona Mardi and the daughter of Bhaiya Murmu of Mandhol village in Gazole Police Station was being negotiated at that time. Saona suggested that the marriage itself might be consummated at Adina Mosque after its occupation. The bride was brought at Adina Mosque. Saona was seated on the throne (the Mimbar) and receiving the bridal garland from the maid-Jitu strolling on the enclosure for the royal family (the Badshah-ki-Takht) and it was at that time that the police fired some blank shots. Saona assured Jitu not to worry about police - the magic incantations of Saona would ere long melt the bulltes of police in water, and bullets would not issue forth from the rifles. Thereafter, Saona addressed the Santals present, urging them to shoot arrows at police. His exhortations and assurances yielded result ; the tribals started shooting arrows at police injuring two constables. Thereafter, the commander of the police team brought Jitu down from the enclosure and started a dialogue with him. The commander assured that fifty bighas of land would be given to him near Pakuahat and a temple would be constructed at government expenditure, if only Jitu did not create disturbance at Adina and left it to itself. The commander was taking enough pains to make Jitu accept the proposal. But Saona was irate. He called at the assembled tribals and incited them, abusing them that they had remained unmoved even though their dear leader was being heckled by police. He urged them again to shoot arrows on the police. The commander also was injured by one of the arrows - as the report goes. Thereafter, the commander issued orders by raising the red flag to open fire on the assembled Santals. As police started firing, the tribals fled. Abul Hossain shot at Jitu killing him.

It is also rumoured that Saona had actually brought about the death of Jitu deliberately. Saona was a Janguru; for some time he had preached the tenets of Ram Sadhu. Reportedly he was a disciple of Ramjit Sadhu and had a strong following in Dinajpur. But evil days befell Saona when he was suspected of moral turpitude involving one of his nearest relations earning him the sobriquet of Dangra Saona. Many of his followers joined the group of Jitu. The erosion of supporters was such that Saona was almost left by himself. Thereafter he also joined the group of Jitu and became a Hindu. But at his heart, he bore grudge against Jitu. Rumour has it that Saona had established contact with the local officers in lieu of monetary considerations, to push Jitu towards death. The administration was also unhappy with Jitu as the ryots had stopped paying rents and abwabs totally on his advice. Thus, this tribal version of the Adina incident sets up Saona Mardi as an agent provocatour, responsible for the death of Jitu.

It may be noticed that Saona had been made responsible for the debacle at Adina Mosque including the idea itself. This myth developed perhaps with the intention of exonerating Jitu of the responsibility of the Adina episode. This will clearly indicate the place of honour for Jitu in the minds of the tribals. With the development of the image of Jitu in matters of social revivalism, the myth of Saona also spread.

A reaction set in the Barind after the killing of Jitu. The resilience put up by the poor tribals in the areas made it impossible to continue agricultural operations. Nobody dared to go to the fields, lest the deadly arrows would fly. But the open movement of Jitu came to a close shortly after his death. A detachment of army carried on flag march through Adina, Gazole, Bamangola, Pakuahat and Habibgpur from 5.1.33 to 12.1.33. With this flag march, the quasi-political Santal movement came to a close. The half-hearted reactions in the area was soon won over by palliative measures taken by the administration.

While considering the movement of Jitu in the Barind, it may be observed that the tribals there were influenced by the non-cooperation movement to some extent. The name of Gandhiji, and the Gandhi Raj, were invoked several times during the decade of the movement. The Santals stopped paying taxes and abwabs in the Barind, as happened elsewhere in the country in course of peasant movements. They had resisted taking over plots of land sold away by courts to the Zamindars and non-agricultural persons. In defiance of orders from the administration, they had looted fish from the beels and jalkars and had plundered crops from the fields which were alienated from them. They had been induced to take the charkha and the more affluent of them had started wearing khadi; the extent was, however, negligible.

In fact, the intensity of the peasant movement in the Barind under the leadership of Jitu was very much discernible till the end of 1924. It may be recalled that the Congress had adopted resolution in November 1921 to advise the peasants to maintain peace, as the Congress would not be in a position to lead the peasant movement which was gradually tending towards violence, in the interest of the national movement. The peasant movements were threatening to cause a rift in the party embodying various strata of the society deriving interest from land. It was observed by Gyan Pandey that the responsibility of maintaining peace was thrust on the peasants whereas the landlords did not receive any such directive nor were they required to concede anything to the peasants [2]. It is apparent that following the resolution, the Congress workers became lukewarm to the peasant movements. It was upto this point of time that the Santals in the Barind remained within the confines of the Gandhiyan way of resistance. Gandhiji's way was passive resistance, Satyagraha to be more precise, and essentially asymmetrical. " More recently, " writes Prof. Galbraith, "the most notable cases of asymmetry in the exercise of countervailing power were those of Mohandas K. (Mahatma) Gandhi in contending with British authority in India, and of his disciple Martin Luther King, Jr., in opposing racial discrimination in the United States. The power of the British in India derived from the carefully cultivated personal images of the Viceroy and the King Emperor or Queen Empress, the similarly cultivated revenue (that is, property) resources of the Raj, and the superb organisation of the Indian Civil and military administration. The compensatory reward for those who were in power or who accepted the social conditioning that urged the benignity of British Rule was not unimportant. But the instrument of prime importance was the threat or reality of condign enforcement from the military and the police.

Against the foregoing elements of British Rule Gandhi offered his powerful personality and a substantial organisation, and from both of these came social conditioning on the right of the Indians to rule themselves. But he did not proceed,as would have been expected, to build an armed force in opposition to that of the British - to bring condign power to bear on condign power. Instead he resorted to non-violence passive resistance to the exercise of British Rule, including at various times resistance to the collection of taxes or the functioning of

---

2. Pandey, Gyan: 'Peasant Revolt and Indian Nationalism; The Peasant movement in Awadh, 1919-22,' in Subaltern Studies I.

the Courts, refusal to obey police orders, and other specific acts of civil disobedience. This departure from the accepted design was a source of infinite wonder, so deeply is symmetry assumed. Nonetheless, the Raj would have dealt in a matter of hours with any army Gandhi might have assembled, while in dealing with this asymmetrical resistance, it was recurrently at a loss and, in the end, defeated[3].

In the backdrop of the foregoing passage, the departure of the Santals in Barind from the Gandhian way would be clear. This departure,however, corresponded with the tribal revivalism. In Jitu, the Santals projected the personality. He built up an organisation (the Satyam Shibam Sect and the Sannyasi Santals) and out of these factors emanated the conditioning power to wrest their own Raj. In 1924, when the peasant movement elsewhere had come to a lull, Jitu started preaching the Santal Raj in Barind. Passive resistance was exercised - including stoppage of rent and abwabs, and refusal to obey orders. But as Jitu attempted at taking recourse to condign power against condign power, he was vanquished to a superior instrument wielding more power. And it was significant that the Santal Raj was preached from a point of time when militant peasant movement was separated from the congress. 'Rajas' or king had been created at other places at the head of the peasant movements in the twenties, particularly following the peasant movements in Awadh, but those were forms of recognition of the personalities around whom the peasants had gathered in the interest of the movement. In the case of Jitu in the Barind, the Santals responded to a desire to revive the traditional 'Golden Age' of the Santals, by establishing the Santal Raj. In Barind, the Santals evinced more of their tribal entity than the peasant identity. And they transcended the limits of peasant movement there.

---

3. Galbraith, J.K. : The Anatomy of Power, pp. 79-80.

Chapter 9

The Appeasement

The storm passed; the rumbling gradually rolled away. But the cloud remained hanging, spreading a gloom of foreboding in the atmosphere. It was surcharged with pent up fury. The swords had been crossed and the tribal was beaten; the loss was grave and he was ruminating how to carry on without the beacon.

The prevailing gloom did not escape the notice of the administration. It embarked on a course of appeasement to mollify the tribals who had been cut to the quick by the death of Jitu. The administration was aware of the sad plight of the tribals and sought to ameliorate by a series of actions.

In June 1933, a Special Officer for the Barind was created. It was proposed that a specially selected Sub-deputy Collector should be vested with the powers of a munsif, and should hear all civil suits against Santals and Oraons at convenient centres in Barind on the basis of the finally published record of rights. Apart from hearing civil suits, the Special Officers would in the course of his touring report to the Collector any matters affecting the Santals,and collect evidence in cases where he would find that rent receipts were not being properly granted. The district administration recommended Shri Kshitis Chandra Berman, Sub-deputy Collector who knew Santali language and who had worked as Attestation Assistant Settlement Officer in Habibpur from 9.10.30. to 15.6.31. Shri Barman fully justified the confidence reposed in him, and by virtue of his work for the Santals, became a living legend hismelf.

Within two years of his assuming charge as Special Officer, Barind, Shri Barman overcame the resistance of the Santals in the interior villages by sheer hard work and good will for the Santals in effecting redress to the poor tribals. Substantial part of the alienated lands were returned to the Santals by the Mahajans and land-lords, and in effecting this change over,

Shri Barman took recourse to executive fiat at times. The unstinted support accorded to him by the successive District Magistrates helped him in achieving his object to a great extent. Santals found a forum to lodge their grievances concerning land and the desired results having obtained, carried Shri Barman to the pinnacle of success and glory to such an extent that Tribal Welfare Officers (posts created subsequently) in the districts of Malda Dinajpur and Jalpaiguri came to be known as Barma Hakim irrespective of their titles. The phenomenon is a rare one in that a cadre of officers was known by an individual officer. Behind the phenomenal success of Shri Barman lay, in part, the positive response of the Santals who sought and found validation of the insurgency in the benign approach of Shri Barman who was essentially a mediator and representative of the Raj. In this context about mediators, the observation of Ranajit Guha may be of some interest. "They (mediators) stood in fact for the political system which dominated the very conditions of the peasant's life and was indeed the object of his revolt. Yet by a curious turn of self-estrangement it was from them rather than from his own will and initiative that he sought validation for his desperate act of defiance. Representatives of the Raj at various levels these mediators came to be regarded by the rebel as source of soverign authority more just and partial towards the peasantry than it was in real life as the custodian of order and protector of landlords, money-lenders and village tyrants of all kinds "[1]. The Santals fondly called Shri K.C. Barman as Barma Hakim. He was addressed as Marang Barma (the elder Barma) and his junior collegue, Shri P.M. Mukherjee was known as Huting Barma (the younger Barma). By the end of 1938, the condition of the Santals improved perceptibly; the oppression by the landlords and Mahajans had almost been stopped. Civil Court notices could not be suppressed and the matter of issuing rent receipts closely watched. Realisation of abwabs was under check to a great extent. The situation improved so much that

1. Guha, Ranajit: Elementary Aspects of Peasant Insurgency in Colonial India, p. 271

the district administration did not feel it necessary to press the earlier recommendation that the Special Officer should be vested with the powers of a munsif to hear all civil suits against Santals and Oraons.

What Barma Hakim could achieve for the Santals was the restoration of alienated land since 1923. And the grateful Santals still remember him.

In ameliorating the condition of the Santals, Barma Hakim did not forget the role of education. He visited most of the primary schools in Barind and perceived the inadequacies. A few changes in teachers were made. The District Inspector of Schools was requested to arrange frequent inspections of the schools. During his tours in the interior, he tried to make the tribals realise the importance of the primary education. He also promised donations to the deserving institutions from the discretionary fund of the District Magistrate, for supplying the more regular students with books, slates and pencils. Distribution of footballs and other playthings to attract children to the schools was also planned. Request was made to appoint a Special Sub-Inspector of Schools to inspect the Santali Schools. It was also felt that the Santal students should know how to read and write their language, apart from Bengali. To that end in view, opening up of a school to impart lessons to the teachers in Santali for about three months was proposed, so that the teachers could instruct the students in Santali in the primary level.

The Parganait system was introduced in Barind in 1934. It was an emulation of the system prevailing in the Santal Parganas. Each Union of Barind had elected a headman (Pargana) and some assistant headman (Desmanjhies) for deciding petty social disputes and working out the instructions of the Special Circle Officer for the Barind Area connected with the schemes for the amelioration of the condition of the Santals. There were 35 Parganas in all, all of them being representative headmen. They were given Sanads signed by the District Magistrate and were given printed instructions for their guidance. Appointments of Parganaits, Desmanjhies and Chakladars (corresponding to

Godets in the village society) were made by the District Magistrate. It was reckoned that the system would be very helpful to the administration. The instructions to the Parganas and the people in general contained the following, among others:-

(a) "In Social matters the Santhals must have to obey the decision of the Parganait.

(b) The bride-price, which was hitherto unlimited, should be Rs. 12 for a virgin girl, Rs. 9 for a widow, and Rs. 7 for a divorced girl.

(c) No divorce should be valid without my (Special Officer's) approval.

(d) Polygamy is discouraged.

(e) Cases of abduction, incest, forcible marriage etc. should be decided according to the social law prevailing in the Santhal Parganas.

The rules prescribed are being enforced by the Parganait"[2].

Once a year, in meeting convened by the administration, Parganas were given various presents like turban, walking-sticks, watches etc. by the District Magistrate in recognition of the services rendered by them. Usually, the expenses were met from the discretionary funds of the District Magistrate. In 1938, it was considered at one stage that the Manjhies might as well be presented with such articles, to create a better atmosphere of cooperation and understanding between the administration and the tribals, and for that end in view, the Divisional Commissioner was approached by the District Magistrate for funds as that would have increased the expenditure to a considerable extent.

Illicit distillation was reportedly checked considerably. Reckless drinking had also come down, as was reported by the

---

2. Barman, K.C.:Report on the Condition of the Santhals in Malda 1934, p. 33

Special Officer. Attempts were made to popularise home-brewing licenses which were granted at Rs. 1-8 each. The Parganas were instructed to help the Excise Sub-Inspectors in securing customers for such licenses. The Commissioner of Excise sanctioned a commission of two annas per rupee (121-1/2 per cent) to those headmen who would sell the licenses. Attempts were also made to waive the stemp-duty of two annas to be levied on the tribal applicants.

Persistent propaganda was made throughout Barind for the improvement of agriculture, introduction of subsidiary crops, such as tobacco, sugarcane, potatoes, ground-nuts, linseed, vegetables, etc., which yielded satisfactory result. The gaurdians were urged to send their wards to school. Constant preaching against the superstitious belief in witches and witch-doctors were being made and much of troubles on the score could be avoided by intercession. The Santals were particularly advised to pay up their rents in time, and without proper receipts, no rent was to be paid. The landlords and their agents and employees were almost forced to stop realising abwabs, and the Special Officer tried his most to accord protection to the tribals against the money-lenders and landlords' agents and employees. Hundreds of cases came to him for arbitration - cases of varying nature and working against tremendous odds, he was able to instil a sense of confidence on him in the minds of the tribals, raising him to the level of a legendary hero. The level of expectation of the tribals from him had been so raised that referring cases to the authorised court would eventually disappoint the tribal thinking that the Barma Hakim had sort of turned him down. But the tribals knew all the same that the Barma Hakim was there to listen to their woes.

Systematic campaign against the money-lenders stiffened their attitude, much to the discomfiture of the tribals. Easier credit-facilities were imperative for the tribals to enable them to continue cultivation. To this end in view, the district administration proposed setting up of a Santal Co-operative Bank for Malda. In February, 1935, the District Magistrate wrote to the Divisional Commissioner outlining the project, requesting for government sanction and grant of Rs. 50,000 only for the proposed bank. Eventually this proposal did not materialise and the Santals fell victim to money lenders, again leading to land alienation.

It is gainsaid that the district administration had been very keen to remove the grievances of the Santals, and saw it fit to recommend new legislations. New posts were created; new proposals were submitted for the benefit of the tribals. The total effect of such administrative steps, perhaps, deserves a scrutiny. Let us take the Parganait system for once.

Inadequacies in legal provisions effected serious limitations to the endeavour of the officials in ameliorating the conditions of the tribals, particularly Santals of Barind. The proposal of creating another non-regulated area like the Santal Parganas did not find favour with the government. Nor did the government agree to take away the tribals from the ambit of civil courts, by empowering the Collector of the district to try all cases where the Santals were involved. In introducing the Parganait system in Barind, the same half-hearted attitude would be apparent. Unlike the Parganas in the Santal Parganas, the Parganas in Barind has no police powers. (The Parganas in the Santal Parganas enjoyed powers of a Sub-Inspector of Police in their respective jurisdictions). In Barind, the Parganas were elected ones and this election had not the social sanction at all places. As we have known, the Pargana is an integral part of the Santal social system and the new Parganas were not evidently the choice of the society. Nor were these Parganas having societal support depending on extensive kinship. We have also known from the statement of Jitu's daughter that there was a Pargana at Salbona on whose death, Biram (Jitu's son) was made a Pargana in 1935, i.e., three years after the death of Jitu. As such, the claim of introducing the Parganait system in Barind would also not stand. What actually was achieved by the district administration was to create a set of people who would maintain a link between the administration and the tribals. Following the incident of

Adina, the relation between the two had been strained. Parganas having been set up in each Union, it was more convenient for the Special Officer to get in touch with them with fair amount of regularity. Yet in Santal society, the importance of the Manjhi is all-pervading and the Manjhi lives in the village. The necessity of winning over the Manjhies was felt by the distict administration as would be evident from the request of the District Magistrate for funds from the Divisional Commissioner to procure persents for the Manjhies along with the Parganas. Incentive for securing candidates for home-brewing licenses granted to the parganas led to pushing of such practice in the village, and did not help in developing healthy atmosphere. It may also be recalled that the tribals had once moved in agitations against such license fee in Midnapur and Malda as well. To be candid, the Parganait system never caught on well. The new leadership had been weak and caught contagion from neighbouring societies. Education was not spreading. Throughout, the conservative traditional leadership was suspicious of the new elites, and did not give way easily.

It may be recalled that the traditional leadership succeeded in retaining the tribal core intact by pursing a rigid course of defensive actions. Witch accusations and trials, often leading to death of the denounced witches, mostly poor women, are manifestations of a defensive social stance. The leadership that emerged at Barind was distinctly apart from the traditional leadership. In the process of re-introduction of the Parganait system, the new elites were transfixed on the tribal society by the administration. It would be seen that the system did not last long and the traditional leadership in the Santal society reverted to its old position, strengthening the Manjhies in the villages. The powers of the Parganas disappeared ere long, probably because the system was considered to be an imposition on the society by the tribals. As long as the new elites were riding with the administration, the traditional leadership kept a low profile. The initial thrust having been over, the traditional leadership once again exerted itself. In the following years, the tribals gradually slided down to their shell and social control over individuals mounted with increasing severity. Over the years, the number of witch accusations and witch-killings increased perceptibly, along with other forms of social control like 'bitlaha' or 'gira' calls. The administration had to relent on occasions. On October 10, 1944, Santals had called a 'bitlaha' affecting the houses of Hopa Santal and Gora Santal, at village Tantibari within Gazole thana, in connection with the illicit sexual intercouse of Hopa Santal with the wife of Chandu Hansda of village Talberia. About ten thousand Santals assembled on the date fixed. Circle Officer Barind visited the spot with the Circle Inspector of Police and some armed constables. The tribals were allowed to continue with the 'bitalaha'.

On another occasion, the Barma Hakim had allowed the tribals to proceed with the projected bitlaha - a non-tribal had taken liberty with a tribal girl. On both the occasions the presence of the Barma Hakim mellowed down the severity of the bitlaha. Eventually the same was the experience of Shri P.M.Mukherjee known as Huting Barma, posted in Dinajpur. Public trials had to be acceded to where the tribal susceptibilities were hurt. These bitlaha or public trials were expressions of tribal solidarity and power, in terms of social control. It is not that the tribals had listened always to the officials who had been working with missionary zeal. They were rather stubborn in their belief in witches and their evil influences on mundane matters.

Attempts at improving upon the moral tone of the tribals through the Parganait system did not succeed. Nor could the parganas motivate the tribals in adopting ideas to improve their lot over mundane matters like how to retain the land, or how best to manage the agriculture on plots of land held by them. In effect, the tribals again lost their land substantially to money-lenders on account of loans necessary for living. This was possible through a system of khai-khalasi or usufructuary mortgages on unregistered deeds. Government failed to effect any system of loans to the tribals through agricultural or co-opertative banks and the achievement of the Barma Hakim was lost in the bargain before long. As the new elites could not bring anything for the community, except a train of control mechanism on behalf of the administration, it lost its sway. Bolstering of the social leadership by introducing Parganait system was thus extremely ephumeral in effect.

The tribals were on the warpath till the end of 1932. Within a decade thereafter, the legend of Barma Hakim pervaded the Santal community in North Bengal. Was this climbing down of the tribe a smooth one, without any remonstration any where ? In at least one incident in 1935, a section of Santals took askance at the approach of the officials urging the tribals to be loyal subjects of the British Raj. In village Mangalpura in Habibpur thana area in November 1935, once Tebra Santal and some others had collected in a meeting to be addressed by the District Magistrate, the Sub-divisional Officer and the Barma Hakim. In that meeting, the Barma Hakim had addressed the tribals and asked them to be loyal subjects whereupon Tebra and his associates raised protest. It is on record that Tebra had assaulted the Barma Hakim for which a criminal case was started against the tribal and he was arrested. Similar incidents had taken place elsewhere and gradually, the resilience of the Santals became muted. The executive actions of the administration tried to improve their lot simultaneously. The natural distrust to the Deko suffered a willing suspension, but the tribals gradually went back to their earlier state of defensive stance.

The second important event that prompted the Santals in forsaking the innovations was the imprisonment of Biram Hembram, a Parganait. Biram was the son of Jitu and he was made a Parganait after three years of Jitu's death. Report goes that one Santal girl was molested by a non-tribal who was produced before the Parganait. It was dark by that time and Biram took the decision to keep the accused at the village, hands and legs bound, to be produced at the police station on the following morning. On production at Court, the man lodged a complaint agaisnt Biram for illegal detention coupled with other charges. Biram was arrested, tried and sent to jail in 1938. And, this incident marked the end of the period of appeasement that the administration had been following since the death of Jitu. With the growing sternness of the administration, the tribals were feeling their way around and that is the time when workers like Sudhendu (Manik) Jha and Nagen Chakraborty started moving among the peasants and forged a unity in the peasant front with the tribals participating wholeheartedly : Barind came to be known as a stronghold of the leftist peasant movement.

The defensive society gradually withdrew itself in the shell of isolation once again. It is not that the war-like attitude had given way all of a sudden. Sustained work had to be done by the Special Officers which eventually paid dividends. There were troubles at various places, but the Special Officers were supported by the Parganas. Tribal Welfare Department was created on 12 June 1952 when Shri K.C. Barman was the Deputy Secretary in the Land and Land Revenue Department.

Epilogue

The imperceptible stream of social consciousness flows underneath, leading the tribe to find out other avenues of self-assertion. It has adopted insurgency as a method to attain its goal. Now it joined other tribal groups in sponsoring the Jharkhand movement, seeking a land and trying to reach new ideas to the tribal society. The traditional leadership has been guarding its prerogative with intense zeal. A conflict between the two sets of elites-old and new - has been raging in the rural areas, leading to loss of life at times. The weakening traditional leadership has been giving way to political power-groups, and new elements are developing in the rural areas who work as intermediaries between such power-groups and the village society. The tribe has already been initiated in the politics of number, and made conscious of its priviliges as a Scheduled Tribe. Unfortunately, most of the privileges are beyond the reach of ordinary tribals living in the rural areas. They have to have a firm agricultural base whereupon the society would rest, and sent out children to the outside world. No viable alternative has so far reached the Santals even through the industrial diversification.

A state of intense anxiety rules in the society. The traditional leadership has been failing perceptibly. Poverty, lack of governmental patronage, increasing pressure from non-tribal neighbours, and such other impediments have been gnawing at the root of his strength. The more enterprising individuals are succumbing to external political baits. With the approach of the new elites, the traditional leadership tended to become apprehensive of social disintegration. As such, there was corresponding reaction in the social body. Long back, the tottering social leadership had devised a group of elites with a counterpoise, the use as a prop in stabilising itself-the system of Janguru and witch was evolved thus - and in the present predicament, the traditional Santal leadership fell for that system once again. Instances of witch-killing or accusations from areas where the Santals have been living in large homogeneous groups are increasing in number. The new elites of the modern times have also been trying to impress the tribal society on the irrelevance of the witch system under the present circumstances. Thus, both the old and the new leadership have been embroiled in a dispute wherein the witch-problem has become the fulcrum. Needless to say that the internal solidarity of the tribe has been adversely affected thereby. The apprehended social disintegration cannot be stopped by enforcing witch-trials in the society. The need of the hour is to devise a programme in which the tribe can participate as a whole. It has to be admitted that the numerical strength of the tribe has been diluted at many a place. The Santals will have to accept the responsibility of much of their actions and maladies, and re-model their pattern of thinking accordingly. Spread of education will definitely help them to appreciate their real difficulties standing on the way of attaining power. A fusion of the traditional and the new elites would greatly facilitate their uphill task. The tribe can no longer ignore the sea of changes around it, and a positive approach to adjust itself to the changed politico-economical circumstances prevailing around is imperative.

A very significant development has already taken place in the life of the tribe. Instead of ushering the 'Personality', it has stood behind the Organisation - an entity beyond the society, the traditional leadership having no control over it. This organisation is projecting leaders who have already started influensing the members of the society; it has already initiated a programme, a movement demanding Jharkhand. New elites have started appearing on the scene, and in times to come, Santal society as a whole, will take part in the movement seeking self-assertion. The new elites would lead the tribe along the new and the national leadership would follow along with other members of the society.

Bibliography

Barman, K.C., Report on the Condition of the Santals in Malda 1934 (Calcutta 1938).

Basak, Radhagobinda, Kautiliya Arthasastra (Calcutta 1964)

Baskey, D.N., Saontal Ganasangramer Itihas (Calcutta 1982)

Board of Revenue, Saontal Birodha Theke Operation, Govt. of West Bengal, Barga, (Calcutta 1980)

Bompas, Cecil Henry, Folklore of the Santal Parganas (London 1909)

Bose, N.K., The Structure of Hindu Society, translated by Andre Beteille (Delhi 1975)

Carter, M.O., Final Report on the Survey and Settlement Operations in the District of Malda, 1928-1935 (Calcutta 1939)

Chakraborty, Rajani Kanta, Gourer Itihas (Malda 1983)

Chakraborty, Sudhir Kumar, Gour Panduar Dharasnane Maldaha (Calcutta-1982)

Chatterjee, Partha. 'Agrarian Relations and Communalism, 1926-35', in R. Guha (ed) Subaltern Studies Vol. I (Delhi 1982)

Chaudhuri, A.B. Witch Killings Amongst Santals (Delhi 1984)

Chaudhuri, A.B., Saontal Samaj, Daini O Bartaman Sankat (Calcutta 1985)

Craig, T.J.A., Report on the Police Administration in the Bengal Presidency for the year 1932 (Calcutta 1933)

Culshaw, W.J. and W.G. Archer, 'The Santal Rebellion', Man in India, Vol. 25(4), December 1945.

Dalton, E.T. Descriptive Ethnology of Bengal (2nd reprint, Calcutta 1973)

Das A.K. and S. Mukhopadhyay, Paschim Banger Adibasi Andolan (Calcutta 1977)

Das Sukumar, Uttarbanger Itihas (Calcutta 1982)

Datta, Bhupendranath, Studies in Indian Social Polity (revised and enlarged edition, Calcutta 1983)

Galbraith, J.K., The Anatomy of Power (Great Britain 1984)

Ghosh, P.K, The Architecture of Gour-Vanga, Vol. I (Calcutta 1977)

Guha, Ranajit, Elementary Aspects of Peasant Insurgency in Colonial India (Delhi 1983)

Habib, Irfan, 'Landed Property in Pre-British India', in R.S. Sarma (ed) Indian Society : Historical Probings (New Delhi 1977)

Hansda, Baidyanath, Mare Hapramko Reak Katha (The Traditions and Institutions of the Santals), translated in Census 1951, West Bengal District Handbooks : Bankura App.V., 1953

Hunter, W.W., The Annals of Rural Bengal (Delhi 1975)

Hutton, J.H., Caste in India (Bombay 1963)

Jha, V. 'From Tribe to Untouchable : The case of Nisadas'in Indian Society : Historical Probings.

Koomar, Rev. C.H., The History of the Santal Parganas, Santals and Paharias (Benageria 1937)

Lahiri, Kalipada, Gour Darpan (Maldah 1982)

Mc Alpin, M.C., Report on the condition of the Santals in the Districts of Birbhum, Bankura, Midnapore and North Balassore (Reprint Calcutta 1981)

Mitra, A., District Handbooks : Malda, Census 1951 (Calcutta 1954)

Moore, Barrinagton, Jr., Social Origins of Dictatorship and Democracy (USA 1966)

O'Malley L.S.S. Bengal District Gazetteers : Bankura (Calcutta 1908)

O'Malley, L.S.S., Bengal District Gazetteers : Sahabad (Calcutta 1906)

O'Malley, L.S.S., History of Bengal, Bihar and Orissa under British Rule (Calcutta 1925)

O'Malley, L.S.S., India's Social Heritage (Delhi 1976)

Orans, Martin, The Santal : A Tribe in Search of A Great Tradition (Detroit 1965)

Pandey, Gyan 'Peasant Revolt and Indian Nationalism : The Peasant Movement in Awadh, 1919-22', in Subaltern Studies, Vol.I

Peterson, J.C.K., Bengal District Gazetteers : Burdwan (Calcutta 1910)

Rasul, M.A., A History of the All India Kisan Sabha (Calcutta 1974)

Ray, Suprakash, Bharater Krishak-Bidroha O Ganatantrik Sangram Vol. I (Calcutta 1966)

Roy U.K. A.K.Das and S.K. Basu, To be with Santals (Calcutta 1982)

Risley, H.H. The Tribes and Castes of Bengal, two volumes (Calcutta 1891).

Sen, Gopinath, Swadhinata Andolane Adibasider Bhumika (Calcutta 1975)

Sengupta J.C. District Gazetteers: Malda 1969

Sharma, R.S. 'Material Milieu of Tantricism', in Indian Society: Historical Probings

Singh, K. Suresh, Dust-strom and Hanging Mist (Calcutta 1966)

Singh, K. Suresh, 'A study in State-Formation Among Tribal Communities' in Indian Society : Historical Probings

Sinha, S.C. 'State Formation and Rajput Myth in Tribal Central India' Man in India, Vol. 42 No. 1 Pp 35-80.

Sinha, S.C. J. Sen and S. Panchbhai, 'The Concept of Diku Among the Tribes of Chotanagpur' Man in India, Vol. 49 (2), April/June 1969, Pp 121-38

Tarkaratna, Panchanan, Kalika Puranam (ed.) (Reprint, Calcutta 1977)

Yinger, Milton J., A Minority Group in American Society (New York 1966)

Index

T